Henry James: A Very Short Introduction

VERY SHORT INTRODUCTIONS are for anyone wanting a stimulating and accessible way into a new subject. They are written by experts, and have been translated into more than 45 different languages.

The series began in 1995, and now covers a wide variety of topics in every discipline. The VSI library currently contains over 650 volumes—a Very Short Introduction to everything from Psychology and Philosophy of Science to American History and Relativity—and continues to grow in every subject area.

Very Short Introductions available now:

ABOLITIONISM Richard S. Newman
THE ABRAHAMIC RELIGIONS
   Charles L. Cohen
ACCOUNTING Christopher Nobes
ADOLESCENCE Peter K. Smith
ADVERTISING Winston Fletcher
AERIAL WARFARE Frank Ledwidge
AESTHETICS Bence Nanay
AFRICAN AMERICAN RELIGION
   Eddie S. Glaude Jr
AFRICAN HISTORY
   John Parker and Richard Rathbone
AFRICAN POLITICS Ian Taylor
AFRICAN RELIGIONS
   Jacob K. Olupona
AGEING Nancy A. Pachana
AGNOSTICISM Robin Le Poidevin
AGRICULTURE Paul Brassley and
   Richard Soffe
ALEXANDER THE GREAT
   Hugh Bowden
ALGEBRA Peter M. Higgins
AMERICAN BUSINESS HISTORY
   Walter A. Friedman
AMERICAN CULTURAL HISTORY
   Eric Avila
AMERICAN FOREIGN RELATIONS
   Andrew Preston
AMERICAN HISTORY Paul S. Boyer
AMERICAN IMMIGRATION
   David A. Gerber
AMERICAN LEGAL HISTORY
   G. Edward White
AMERICAN MILITARY HISTORY
   Joseph T. Glatthaar

AMERICAN NAVAL
   HISTORY Craig L. Symonds
AMERICAN POLITICAL
   HISTORY Donald Critchlow
AMERICAN POLITICAL PARTIES
   AND ELECTIONS L. Sandy Maisel
AMERICAN POLITICS
   Richard M. Valelly
THE AMERICAN PRESIDENCY
   Charles O. Jones
THE AMERICAN REVOLUTION
   Robert J. Allison
AMERICAN SLAVERY
   Heather Andrea Williams
THE AMERICAN SOUTH
   Charles Reagan Wilson
THE AMERICAN WEST Stephen Aron
AMERICAN WOMEN'S HISTORY
   Susan Ware
AMPHIBIANS T. S. Kemp
ANAESTHESIA Aidan O'Donnell
ANALYTIC PHILOSOPHY
   Michael Beaney
ANARCHISM Colin Ward
ANCIENT ASSYRIA Karen Radner
ANCIENT EGYPT Ian Shaw
ANCIENT EGYPTIAN ART AND
   ARCHITECTURE Christina Riggs
ANCIENT GREECE Paul Cartledge
THE ANCIENT NEAR EAST
   Amanda H. Podany
ANCIENT PHILOSOPHY
   Julia Annas
ANCIENT WARFARE
   Harry Sidebottom

For more information visit our website

www.oup.com/vsi/

Susan L. Mizruchi

HENRY JAMES

A Very Short Introduction

OXFORD
UNIVERSITY PRESS

OXFORD
UNIVERSITY PRESS

Oxford University Press is a department of the University of Oxford.
It furthers the University's objective of excellence in research, scholarship,
and education by publishing worldwide. Oxford is a registered trade mark of
Oxford University Press in the UK and certain other countries.

Published in the United States of America by Oxford University Press
198 Madison Avenue, New York, NY 10016, United States of America.

Library of Congress Cataloging-in-Publication Data

Names: Mizruchi, Susan L. (Susan Laura), author.
Title: Henry James : a very short introduction / Susan L. Mizruchi.
Description: New York, NY : Oxford University Press, [2021] | Series:
Very short introductions | Includes bibliographical references and index.
Identifiers: LCCN 2020050088 (print) | LCCN 2020050089 (ebook) |
ISBN 9780190944384 (paperback) | ISBN 9780190944407 (epub)
Subjects: LCSH: James, Henry, 1843–1916—Criticism and interpretation.
Classification: LCC PS2124 .M59 2021 (print) | LCC PS2124 (ebook) |
DDC 813/.4—dc23
LC record available at https://lccn.loc.gov/2020050088
LC ebook record available at https://lccn.loc.gov/2020050089

3 5 7 9 8 6 4 2

Printed in Great Britain by Ashford Colour Press Ltd., Gosport, Hants.,
on acid-free paper

To Sascha: A little book for the light of my life

Contents

List of illustrations

Prologue

There is no passage more exemplary of Henry James's writings than the description of afternoon tea that opens *The Portrait of a Lady*:

Under certain circumstances there are few hours in life more agreeable than the hour dedicated to the ceremony known as afternoon tea. There are circumstances in which, whether you partake of the tea or not—some people of course never do—the situation is in itself delightful. Those that I have in mind in beginning to unfold this simple history offered an admirable setting to an innocent pastime. The implements of the little feast had been disposed upon the lawn of an old English country house in what I should call the perfect middle of a splendid summer afternoon. Part of the afternoon had waned, but much of it was left, and what was left was of the finest and rarest quality. Real dusk would not arrive for many hours; but the flood of summer light had begun to ebb, the air had grown mellow, the shadows were long upon the smooth, dense turf. They lengthened slowly, however, and the scene expressed that sense of leisure still to come which is perhaps the chief source of one's enjoyments of such a scene at such an hour. From five o'clock to eight is on certain occasions a little eternity; but on such an occasion as this the interval could be only an eternity of pleasure. The persons concerned in it were taking their pleasure quietly, and they were not of the sex which is supposed to furnish the regular votaries of the ceremony I have mentioned. The shadows on the perfect lawn were straight and angular; they were the shadows of an old man sitting in a deep wicker-chair near the low table on which the tea had been served, and of two younger men strolling to and fro, in desultory talk, in front of him. The old man had his cup in his hand; it was an unusually large cup, of a different pattern from the rest of the set and painted in brilliant colours. He disposed of its contents with much circumspection, holding it for a long time close to his chin, with his face turned to the house. His companions had either finished their tea or were indifferent to their privilege; they smoked cigarettes as they continued to stroll. One of them, from time to time, as he passed, looked with a certain attention at the elder man, who unconscious of observation, rested his eyes upon the rich red front of his dwelling. The house that rose beyond the lawn was a structure to repay such consideration and was the most characteristic object in the peculiarly English picture I have attempted to sketch (5).

The scene stages the rituals of a privileged class: people in the position to enjoy their leisure on a summer afternoon on the lawn of an English country house. Anyone ambivalent about a class system or worried about social inequality might be put off by the air of entitlement and the way the passage seems to celebrate the ceremonial pleasures of the elite. Yet the role the omniscient narrator plays here in relieving the potential for smugness is important. His gently humorous exaggerations reinforce the peacefulness and glow of their lives ("delightful," "admirable," "perfect," "splendid," "finest," "rarest"), but also create distance between the characters and readers.

The rhetoric invites us to imagine afternoon tea as the rite of a strange tribe, meriting careful observation and classification. While presumably enviable, the leisure class participating in this custom is as mysterious as any other human group. A sign of their mystery is that we are introduced to "shadows" before people, ("the shadows were long upon the smooth, dense turf…shadows

1. **This photograph of an English country house, taken by the noted early twentieth-century photographer Alvin Langdon Coburn, was used as the frontispiece to the first volume of the New York Edition of James's *The Portrait of a Lady*. It evokes the novel's European setting, as reflected through Coburn's American lens.**

of an old man... and of two younger men"). The outline or figure *precedes* the person, suggesting the challenge of accessing human beings. It takes time to fathom depths in those we encounter, and a crucial part of the story will be what the protagonist Isabel Archer *misses* about those who determine her fate.

Readers will benefit from the omniscient narrator's guidance, which is already part of the story, for the style—the shower of adjectives, the qualifications, the sheer precision—calls attention to point of view, observation, and to the particular observer who is "sketch[ing]" this "peculiarly English scene." James invokes the personal pronoun no fewer than four times, referring to the

3

narrator's "mind," his turn of phrase ("what I should call"), his past ("I have mentioned"), and his effort to picture the scene ("I have attempted to sketch"). And however playful, the sensibility of this self-conscious narrator is moral, with the terms "innocence" and "perfection" hinting that we have begun in Eden but are about to fall into a narrative of tragic knowledge. What other reason is there to read if not to experience vicariously the suffering of engaging but flawed human characters?

Despite the emphasis on pleasure and ease, the unmistakable foreboding promises that there is misery to come. The metaphor of an afternoon where "the flood of summer light had begun to ebb" the mellowing air, and the "old man" whose condition absorbs the "attention" of one of the younger suggest that the man's days are numbered, his death imminent. It should not be lost on us that this elder is the owner of the stately mansion ("his dwelling"), which implies a considerable fortune, and that inheritance, the transmission of wealth, is as imminent as death itself. The characterization of the talk of the younger men as "desultory," along with the fact that they are "indifferent" to the ceremony as they "stroll" smoking, suggests that they are aimless. Both of these young men will need, like the rest of us, some drama to keep them motivated and entertained.

It will be a drama heightened by aesthetic self-consciousness, where the artist and his art will be of perpetual interest. These subjects are hallmarks of James's writing, as are the conventions and etiquette of the social elite; the lives of transplanted Americans abroad—two of the three men in this prototypical English scene are American—; the prominence of mental action; and a tendency toward narrative detachment that James shared with contemporary ethnographers, whose terms and methods punctuate his work. The ethnographic cast of James's imagination is evident both formally, in his use of metaphors and stylistic devices (e.g., the emphasis on the observer's standpoint), and thematically, in his subject matter and ideas.

4

The most distinctive feature of James's novels is accentuated by its absence; the woman or female center is missing from her customary place ("regular votaries") presiding over the tea table. Delaying the protagonist's entrance is a common novelistic strategy for heightening suspense (as in the delayed introductions of Ahab in Melville's *Moby-Dick* or Gatsby in Fitzgerald's *The Great Gatsby*). In this instance it also foreshadows the female protagonist's resistance to convention. Foiling expectation is a vital trait of Isabel Archer. The tension between her desire to be free and the designs of those she encounters provides the plot: the story "of a certain young woman affronting her destiny."

This line is from the novel's preface, which James wrote in 1908 when he revised *The Portrait of a Lady* and other major novels for a definitive New York Edition of his work, and wrote prefaces to each. Noting in that same preface how previous writers, such as Charles Dickens, Sir Walter Scott, and Robert Louis Stevenson, avoided centering their fictions on women, James distinguishes himself by his choice to embrace "the wonder" that "as we look at the world how absolutely, how inordinately, the Isabel Archers…insist on mattering." While this could be understood as condescending, and other references by James in this preface and elsewhere to the "frail vessels" who thrust their importance upon the world heightens such concerns, we should notice that this mildly deflating humor is consistent with the opening description of the tea ceremony. The point is that James includes himself and his project in the effacement of his central subject. It is his habit to deny the seriousness of what he and his narrative alter-egos clearly regard as momentous. For James there is nothing more significant than the situations of women and girls, nor is there any vocation more serious than the art of perceiving and recreating those situations and the more general experience of social beings in complex literary prose.

While James is notorious for equivocation and verbosity, what is remarkable about this passage is the economy with which he manages in a single paragraph to touch upon all the principal concerns of the novel.

Like this concise description of afternoon tea, my book is a "very short introduction" to a big subject. Henry James was a prolific writer for most of his adulthood. Considered to be among the greatest English-language novelists, he was nominated for a Nobel Prize three times during his life and specialized in profound portraits of human character, the relations between genders, moral conflicts, and the myriad cruelties—psychological and social—that prevailed in modern middle- and upper-class society. He wrote with extraordinary insight about women and girls, and about the power conferred by money and the vulnerability conferred by lacking it. In an era of professionalization, James was the author as consummate professional, publishing over a forty-five-year career a voluminous collection of novels, stories, plays, travel narratives, autobiographies, biographies, literary criticism, reviews, and ten thousand letters—a number that excludes the many he destroyed to preserve his privacy.

Fellow writer William Dean Howells's remark that James was not "a novelist...after the old fashion, or after any fashion but his own," confirms the uniqueness of James's literary achievement. Yet there may be no major American author who has been more subject to parody and dismissal. While James's distinguished body of work is difficult to avoid, straddling as it does the late nineteenth-century transition from realism to modernism, and covering every literary genre, assessments of James run along lines of taste. Readers either love or hate him, and those in the latter camp often seem to have monopolized the best lines. His brother William complained that his novels "reversed every traditional canon of storytelling, especially the fundamental one of telling the story!" One literature professor confessed an exasperation felt by many: "I never read a James novel that I did not want to hurl across the room when I finished." This has something to do with tone. Some Jamesian pronouncements seem ripe for caricature, such as "Try to be one on whom nothing is lost." The novelist Donald Barthelme takes the bait in *Snow White*, advising, "Try to be one of the people about whom nothing is known." As one of his most sympathetic critics, Ruth Yeazell, observed, "James's mastery has sometimes placed him under suspicion."

But it is above all the idea that James's writing is difficult and obscure, marked by long convoluted sentences and abstract diction, that has earned him the reputation of the most rarefied English-language author. Another sympathetic critic, Seymour Chatman, has noted that "it is hard to think of an occasion in a novel by James when a real taste is tasted or a real smell smelled." In fact, there are two dogs in the first scene of *Portrait of a Lady*, each lovingly detailed: "a beautiful collie...watching the master's face almost as tenderly as the master took in the still more magisterial physiognomy of the house," and "a bristling bustling terrier bestow[ing] a desultory attendance upon the...gentleman." Chatman goes on to show how richly colloquial James's language is—a colloquialism that reveals his interest in "the actual sounds made by the society that he so studiously observed."

Indeed, the majority of James's metaphors are commonplace, a method that James used deliberately, increasing the incidence of idioms in the revisions he made for his New York Edition novels. James knew that was the window to his society, that ordinary speech was hackneyed, not rare and poetic. Though much has been made of James's "late style," the differences between his early and later works are more gradual than this suggests. As James grew in confidence as a writer, developing his theories about character and language, and his techniques for representing them, his fictions evolved accordingly, becoming ever more complex accounts of human experience. James's "late style" is simply his best and most mature narrative method, writing, he said, "that could bear without cracking the strongest pressure we throw on

7

it." This is why an early masterpiece like *The Portrait of a Lady* (1881) shares most of the linguistic features of the work typically classified as "late."

The issue of James's nationality is also controversial. His naturalization as a British citizen seven months before he died on February 28, 1916, has led to misconceptions about his relationship to his home country. James became a British national during World War I, when he was obligated to register as an alien, despite his allegiance to the Allies and his inability, as he wrote to his agent James Pinker, "to care for anything but what happens to…our armies." Yet he left careful instructions that his ashes be buried in the cemetery of Cambridge, Massachusetts, beside those of his parents, his brother William, and his sister, Alice.

James was an American with cosmopolitan sensibilities, which he viewed as essential to the modern writer. In his 1879 biography of Nathaniel Hawthorne, he contrasted his predecessor with the "more Europeanized" American writer of today, who would "inevitably accommodate himself more easily to the idiosyncrasies of foreign lands." This was partly owing to the Civil War, which had "introduced into the national consciousness a certain sense of proportion and relation, of the world being a more complicated place.…The good American, in days to come, will be a more critical person…[having] eaten of the tree of knowledge.…He will be without discredit to his well-known capacity for action, an observer." James's conviction that literary innovation in the modern era demanded an openness to the expanding borders of societies and nations was realized in the way he pursued models for his craft, absorbing ideas and examples from everywhere. A reliable account of his professional development requires attention to multiple contexts and influences—American, British, French, and Russian.

James embraced a process of self-initiation to become a writer, which involved traveling and observing, reading and reviewing,

8

cultivating editors and publishers, and testing his own literary mettle by experimenting with various prose genres. But no testing ground was more powerful than that of the James family itself. As William observed of his brother Henry, "He is a native of the James family, and has no other country." His starting point in a family of ambitious intellectuals with ties to some of the most formidable figures of mid-nineteenth-century America provided a critical laboratory for his illustrious career.

A standard biography that appears in many editions of James's writings tells us that he was "such an inveterate diner-out" after moving to London for good in the winter of 1878–79, that he confessed to accepting 107 dinner invitations. Yet understanding James means accessing parts of him he kept sequestered, despite his sociability. Substantial archival research enables biographer Lyndall Gordan's recognition that "the social Henry James…a good fellow who enjoys company and goes out of his way for other people…blocks from our sight a stranger character, extremely private and fiercely ambitious, who had scruples but could be ruthless when privacy or ambition was thwarted…James wasn't idling in great houses. He was inspecting his material." This warning is supported by brother William's comment that Henry lived "hidden in the midst of his alien manners—assumed as 'protective resemblances'—like a marine crustacean draped in 'rich sea weeds and rigid barnacles.'"

Another reminder of James's depths comes in *A Small Boy and Others*, where he describes the year the family lived in London, and how the brothers, then fourteen and fifteen, were left to their own devices, wandering the city attending plays and visiting museums and exhibitions. One event they took in was the Academy Show of 1858 featuring Pre-Raphaelite painters. "The very word Pre-Raphaelite wore for us that intensity of meaning, not less than of mystery, that thrills us in its perfection but for one season, the prime hour of first initiations," James wrote. But he was impressed by "Holman Hunt's Scapegoat most of all, which

2. William Holman Hunt's dramatic painting *The Scapegoat*, begun on location near the Dead Sea, was completed in London in 1856. James saw it in London at a special exhibition of Pre-Raphaelite paintings when he was in his teens, and he was haunted by it.

I remember finding so charged with the awful that I was glad I saw it in company—*it* in company and I the same: I believed, or tried to believe, I should have feared to face it all alone in a room."

Anyone familiar with the painting of the exiled creature staggering alone in the desert, horns bound in red cloth, parched mouth, one desperate eye registering consciousness of its doom, can imagine how it might have terrified a sensitive adolescent with his own emerging sense of difference from others, and from his sturdy older brother in particular. The anecdote joins adolescent initiation and sacrificial exile, while contrasting individual isolation with the comforts of "company." It also suggests the necessity of social protections for those who are vulnerable, foregrounding a preternatural awareness on James's part of the outsider status that he would embrace as his own and make the vibrant source of his art.

Chapter 1
Becoming Henry James

Henry James Jr. was born on April 15, 1843, in Washington Square in New York City. His parents were of Irish (father) and Scots-Irish (mother) descent. James's mother, Mary Walsh, had grown up in a wealthy Manhattan family, and his father was the son of a banker in Albany, New York, who had provided Henry Sr. with the means to live as a lecturer and philosopher of Swedenborgianism. Arriving in America, in the words of his grandson William, with only "a very small sum of money [and] a Latin grammar," William James, the Albany banker, was a classic American success story. Transitioning from master of a tobacco shop, to operator of an express business, to real estate and utilities mogul, he became a benefactor of the Erie Canal as well as of Union College. His son Henry resisted his father's entrepreneurial acumen despite benefitting from it. As his own son, the writer Henry James, later noted, "The rupture with my grandfather's tradition and attitude was complete; we were never in a single case, I think, for two generations, guilty of a stroke of business."

And yet the fact that "Billy James," as he was called, had "literally bought Syracuse…with a shrewd eye to its salt springs" ensured that his grandson the novelist would enjoy "the spoils of Syracuse…through much of his writing career." Moreover, Billy James's work ethic and sense of purpose was transmitted along with his wealth, though even the son's philosophy expressed a preference for *being* over *doing*. William Dean Howells remarked of Henry Sr.'s most renowned work, *The Secret of Swedenborg*, that the author "had kept the secret very well." Henry Sr. was a member of the New England intelligentsia, a friend of Horace Greeley, the newspaper editor, and Ralph Waldo Emerson, the philosopher, and of Transcendentalists such as Margaret Fuller and Bronson Alcott. When he traveled abroad, these ties produced introductions to British literary luminaries such as Thomas Carlyle and William Thackeray. The writer Henry David Thoreau paid a legendary call to the James family when Henry Jr. was an infant, and Emerson responded to the news of Henry Jr.'s birth by congratulating Mrs. James "on the new friend, though little now, who has come to her hearth."

Henry was preceded by a brother, William, born in January 1842, who became a leading American philosopher of the Pragmatist tradition and a professor of the new science of psychology at Harvard. One of Henry's earliest memories was "of my brother's occupying a place in the world to which I couldn't at all aspire... as if he had gained such an advance of me in his sixteen months' experience of the world before mine began that I never for all the time of childhood and youth in the least caught up with him or overtook him." Henry's omission of adulthood from the competition with his brother suggests that he believed himself eventually to have caught up. But in childhood and youth, Henry's feelings of loss in relation to William were pronounced, and inflected in particular by the impression of his sibling's greater virility. Henry described how his offer of companionship was once dismissed by his older brother with the remark, "*I* play with boys who curse and swear!" Henry's recognition that "I simply wasn't qualified," and subsequent admission that he found "all boys... difficult to play with," led to refuge in his own pursuits, which tended to involve "literary" and "pictorial composition."

But if Henry had difficulties keeping up with William, the situation of the three James siblings born after Henry was even more challenging. Garth Wilkinson, Robertson, and Alice, the youngest, born in 1845, 1846, and 1848, respectively, all struggled with the examples of their gifted elder siblings in a family where intellectual achievement was the criterion of worth. The journalist and editor E. L. Godkin reported that "there could not be a more entertaining treat than a dinner at the James house, when all the young people were at home. They were full of stories of the oddest kind, and discussed questions of morals or taste or literature with a vociferous vigor so great as sometimes to lead the young men to leave their seats and gesticulate on the floor." However "entertaining" for guests, the anecdote confirms how contentious familial debates could be, and how much it mattered for those involved to emerge with their self-respect intact.

The disputatious atmosphere of family life was partly the product of the nineteenth-century American society in which Henry James and his siblings grew up—a world of reformers and reform, with every man, Emerson said derisively, "a draft of a new Community in his waistcoat pocket." Henry Senior was a full participant, someone who "believed in believing," especially in the power of society to realize the virtue in humanity, under the best circumstances. He wrote that "a true society would guarantee to every man, woman, and child, for the whole term of his natural life, food, clothing, shelter, and the opportunities of an education adapted to his tastes." His theory that "the measure of a man's goodness is his use to society" was passed on to his talented offspring, who grew up convinced that they were required to contribute something important to the world.

Henry Sr. also transmitted his eloquence, in person and on paper. The James family biographer, F.O. Matthiessen, writes, "The most enduring influence from their father was his gift of language…there are many witnesses to how Henry Senior's extraordinary command of rhetoric induced in his children a

13

ready emulation." Given his prominence as a literary arbiter, E. L. Godkin's observation, "I suppose there was not in his day a more formidable master of English style," was noteworthy. But Henry Sr.'s primary legacy was his modeling of intellectual life. There was nothing, the James offspring were taught, more valuable or noble. And while Henry Sr. was aware of the good fortune that enabled his devotion to the life of the mind, he made clear to his sons that commerce itself and a commercial approach to any endeavor was to be repudiated. "I desire my child to become an upright man, a man in whom goodness shall be induced not by mercenary motives," he wrote, "as I know that this character or disposition cannot be forcibly imposed upon him, but must be freely assumed, I surround him as far as possible with an atmosphere of freedom."

Henry Sr.'s ideal of freedom guided the education he devised for his children. It involved, first of all, an extended period in Europe from 1855 to 1860, when the family lived successively in England, France, Switzerland, and Germany. The children were exposed to art, architecture, and theater, learned French and German, and were encouraged to read avidly, while receiving little formal schooling. But even during the early years in America, the children had been mostly freed from attending school, or so disrupted in their experiences of it as to make it pale beside familial influences. It was their father's viewpoint, rather than any fruits of a larger educational system, that made a lasting imprint on their minds. While Henry Sr. "delight[ed] ever in the truth," his namesake wrote, he was "generously contemptuous of the facts ... [so] the literal played in our education as small a part as it perhaps ever played in any, and we wholeheartedly breathed inconsistency and ate and drank contradictions."

The same was true of their religious training. The James children were urged to worship with a sense of liberality, to visit a variety of churches with the thought "that there was no communion, even that of the Catholics, even that of the Jews, even that of the

3. This daguerreotype of Henry James Sr. and Henry James Jr. was taken in 1854 by the renowned Civil War photographer Matthew Brady in his New York studio, when the future author was eleven years old.

Swedenborgians, from which we need find ourselves excluded." Henry Jr. wished "that there might have been either much less religion or much more so." Given the scholarliness of the family, that they lived for a time on Quincy Street in Cambridge blocks away from Harvard, and that many of their peers studied there, the fact that neither William nor Henry Jr. were Harvard undergraduates confirms their father's unconventional attitudes toward academia. William was eventually a student at Harvard's medical school, and Henry had a brief sojourn at Harvard Law School, which solidified his conviction of a literary vocation. In 1862–63, James was "a singularly alien" member of the first-year class, "systematically faithful" to the law lectures without "understanding the first word of what they were about."

Henry Sr.'s efforts to cultivate his children intellectually, spiritually, and morally were exclusive to his sons. Despite possessing an intellect on a par with William and Henry, their sister, Alice, was left out, while his wife, Mary, was lauded as a self-sacrificing caregiver. Henry Sr. wrote that woman's virtue "disqualifies her for all didactic dignity. Learning and wisdom do not become her." Mary James seems to have been a relatively placid person, willing to subordinate herself to the family men, but her example could not have been less suited to Alice, and a life of invalidism seems to have been the result. Because William and Henry were also invalids for substantial intervals in their lives, it is possible that Mary James was less content than her husband believed, and cultivated helplessness in her offspring to establish her own necessity.

The Civil War extended the harsh politics of the James family. William enlisted in 1862, but somehow managed to leave the military after a few months. Henry was drafted and also eventually released from duty. Henry Sr. approved his older sons' retreat from service, while pressing the two younger, Wilky and Bob, to enlist. Offering up the younger sons as emblems of their commitment to abolitionism, the Jameses protected the eldest by sanctioning the claims of illness that ultimately freed both from the bloody battle. Still, however much he was valued at home, Henry Jr. had to come to terms with failing the era's tests of

4. This photograph of Henry James is believed to have been taken in Newport, Rhode Island, in 1863, when James was a student at Harvard Law School. James was only twenty years old at the time, and he published his first short story a year later.

manhood: his inability to thrive in law school and avoidance of the war that was consuming the lives of many young men he knew, including his younger brothers.

Henry Jr.'s ambivalent relationship to conventional masculinity enhanced his sensitivity toward his sister, Alice, five years his junior. Throughout their lives, Henry and Alice felt a deeper kinship with each other, emotionally and intellectually, than they did with their other siblings. William, as the eldest son, identified with his father while Wilky and Bob were bound together both by age and by their sense of exclusion from the family business of intellectual attainment. Henry's appreciation of Alice, his closeness to her, was a forerunner of his lifelong attraction to strong, intelligent women. As a London friend noted of him, he "seemed to look at women rather as women look at them. Women look at women as persons; men look at them as women. The quality of sex in women, which is their first and chief attraction to most men, was not their chief attraction to James."

His attraction to a life of letters that was controlled by men but often viewed as the domain of women was the ultimate sign of his difference. But James had the strength of character and the courage to understand where his own talents lay, and to pursue them with a determination that was to distinguish his entire professional life. Within a year he had published an unsigned story, "The Tragedy of Errors" (February 1864) and another that was signed "The Story of a Year" in the *Atlantic Monthly* (March 1865), and he launched himself on the career that would establish him as among the great fictionalizers of women's experience and foremost novelists in English.

The literary scene that Henry James entered in the mid-1860s was ruled by E. L. Godkin, editor of the *Nation*, Charles Eliot Norton, editor of the *North American Review*, and James T. Fields, editor of the *Atlantic*, who, with his wife, Annie, ran a Boston salon that hosted local and foreign literary lights,

5. Henry James enjoyed drawing, though he was more of a dabbler than his brother William, who studied art seriously. Henry included this sketch of his sister, Alice, in a May 23, 1872, letter to his parents. Henry and Alice had a close relationship, and he commented upon reading her diary after her death that it demonstrated her "energy and personality of intellectual and moral being."

Stowe and Dickens among them. James's family connections ensured his welcome at the Fields's home, and he was soon dining with Stowe, and launched as a promising new voice on the cultural scene. The alacrity of James's success was striking by any standard: before the age of twenty-two, his work had appeared in leading American magazines. His métier at the beginning was reviewing, where the critical wit honed at the family dinner table was put to use.

An 1865 review in the *Nation* of Whitman's *Drum Taps* was notable for its disdain: "It has been a melancholy task to read this book; and it is still a more melancholy one to write about it," the review began. Among its choice comments: "The frequent capitals are the only marks of verse in Mr. Whitman's writing. There is, fortunately, but one attempt at rhyme"; "Very good poetry has come out of prose before this. To this we would reply that it must first have gone into it"; "To become adopted as a national poet, it is not enough to discard everything in particular and to accept everything in general, to amass crudity upon crudity, to discharge the undigested contents of your blotting-book into the lap of the public. You must respect the public which you address; for it has taste, if you have not."

James's views of Whitman would soften over time, culminating in Edith Wharton's memory of his marvelous recitation of *Leaves of Grass* during a 1905 visit to her Lenox home: "I had never before heard poetry read as he read it; and I never have since. He chanted it, and he was not afraid to chant it." James told Wharton that Whitman was "undoubtedly a very great genius." Only the added point that "one cannot help deploring his too-extensive acquaintance with the foreign languages" reminds us that this appreciative old man was a mellower version of the fierce young critic.

James's youthful reviews reflected the magnitude of his ambition. His desire to be a leading figure in American letters made him especially hard on compatriots. These aspirations were a family affair. His father managed his business with American publishers after he moved to England, and his mother stayed abreast of his sales, urging him in 1872 to "find a brisker market" for his work than afforded by the *Atlantic* and the *Nation*. Parental interest in his finances was explained in part by the fact that, through the 1880s, James lived primarily on his earnings as a writer. It was not until the 1890s, and the 1892 death of his sister Alice in particular, which resulted in her portion of the family inheritance reverting to him, that James's livelihood was significantly enhanced by family funds.

His relationship to the literary marketplace was characteristically ambivalent: in an 1872 letter to brother William, James complained that "the multitude has absolutely no taste—none at least that a thinking man is bound to defer to. To write for the few who have is doubtless to lose money—but I am not afraid of starving." As that prophet of the literary scene William Dean Howells had predicted in 1867, the idiosyncrasies of James's writing would require him to "in a very great degree create his audience."

Yet despite his reservations about the marketplace, James was from the beginning a shrewd promoter of his own work. Among the first literary authors to navigate the international publishing scene effectively, he managed to profit from the security of American copyright law and the ambiguity of British law, sometimes forcing American and British editors to compete for his writings. Success for James meant the acclaim of popular as well as highbrow readers, the ability to support himself respectably through his writings, and worldwide recognition. *Daisy Miller* (1878) was James's first taste of the kind of success he craved. "Everyone is talking about it," he wrote from England to William. "Its success has encouraged me as regards the faculty of appreciation of the English public for the thing is sufficiently subtle, yet people appear to have comprehended it. It has given me a capital start here, and in future I shall publish all my things in English magazines . . . and sell advanced sheets in America; thereby doubling my profits."

What did assist James's career immensely was the growth of the publishing industry in the post–Civil War period, especially periodical publishing, catalyzed by the expansion and professionalization of advertising. The practice that proved most beneficial to James's earnings was serialization, where novels were introduced through installments in periodicals, which created an audience for the subsequent book. Almost all serious novelists of the time published their narratives first in serial form. Historians of the book have tended to focus on top-selling books, thus overlooking the outsized role played by magazines in the careers of professional writers such as James, who managed to bolster their steady if not spectacular earnings by placing their fiction in magazines prior to their appearance as novels. During a congressional committee hearing on copyright, a publisher asserted, "If it were not for that one saving opportunity of the great American magazines, which are now the leading ones of the world and have an international reputation and circulation, American authorship would be at a still lower ebb than at present."

Despite James's skills in negotiating the literary marketplace and the fact that male publishers controlled it in the United States and in England, James nursed a lifelong resentment of women writers he believed unjustly rewarded by a reading public that eluded him. Like his forebear Nathaniel Hawthorne, James could be exceptionally empathic about the limits upon women in literature and in life. In an 1868 piece on "Modern Women" for the *Nation*, James attacked the marriage market and anticipated greater freedoms for women in the future. Yet also in keeping with Hawthorne, James could be dismissive of women writers he competed against professionally.

James's hostile review of Louisa May Alcott's novel *Moods* in the *North American Review* (1865) confirmed how much his first novel, *Watch and Ward*, serialized in the *Atlantic Monthly* (1871), echoed it in portraying an orphan raised by a guardian who eventually marries her. James's fascination with the Pygmalion theme and with the overbearing attachments of family life—those between siblings as well as those between parents and children—is a constant in his writings, and represent important continuities with more popular fiction by women. James's first great work, *The Portrait of a Lady*, critiques the incest paradigm by exploring its impact on an original and independent heroine.

Like all great writers, James took from everywhere and could be strident toward those from whom he took most. The first "grown-up novel" James recalled reading was *The Lamplighter* (1854) by Maria Cummins. During his first decade as a literary professional, he wrote reviews of books such as Susan Warner's *The Wide, Wide World* and Harriet Beecher Stowe's *Uncle Tom's Cabin*, because their work dominated the magazines and novel sales. In some cases, as in his review of Elizabeth Stoddard's *The Morgesons* (1862), James's animus was so pronounced that the *North American Review* rejected it; other reviews, like that of Anne Moncure Crane's *Opportunity* (1867), were more generous.

These predecessors embraced subjects that would be central to James's own fictions: the validation of emotions and interior reflection, the focus on bonds among women, the attention to female development and the inner lives of girls, the psychology of submission and abjection, and the resistance to such self-effacement displayed by extraordinary characters. In works by writers such as Warner and Stowe, intimacy can be dangerous: parents, siblings, lovers, and confidants set up house in the soul, cultivating submission from within. There was nothing that interested James more, and in creating characters such as Madame Merle and Isabel Archer of *The Portrait of a Lady* he picked up the baton from the Sentimentalists and flew.

Abjection came naturally to James. It was a family style he understood deeply and appropriated as a deliberate affect. This is particularly evident in Henry's relationship to his brother William. In letters and in his autobiographies, Henry embraces abjection while foregrounding his brother William's greater masculinity and success, a stance that minimizes William's psychological fragility and struggles to settle on a vocation. In fact, Henry's path to a profession that would engage all of his talent and skill was comparatively direct and effortless. Close their whole lives, sharing experiences, obligations, memories, as well as ideas, what was remarkable about the James brothers was how antithetical their intellects were.

Both Henry and William were shaped by their father's morality, and believed in their obligation to contribute to the social good. But their relationship to the commercial spirit of their native land was notably different. William's philosophy was sincerely engaged with American ideals of enterprise and innovation, whereas Henry's fiction evinced an increasing ironic attitude toward these ideals, both thematically and formally. Indeed, no fiction writer of the time was more passionately devoted to representing the dire consequences of human beings exploiting others for self-advancement or profit.

In their exchanges on each other's work, Henry tended toward reticence, doubting his ability to judge William's science, whereas William liberally appraised Henry's fiction. This did not mean that Henry ignored William's work. In a letter from 1907, Henry reported that his reading of William's book *Pragmatism* was "really the event of my summer." His consistent reading of what his brother produced made his knowledge of social scientific principles prodigious, something that is often overlooked by Henry's critics. One of William's chief objections to Henry's fiction had to do with its abstractness. He described himself as "struck unfavorably by the tendency of the personages to reflect on themselves and give an acute critical scientific introspective classification of their own natures and states of mind." In another letter to Henry, William was effusive about Hawthorne's *The House of the Seven Gables*, adding, "It tickled my national feeling not a little to note the resemblance of Hawthorne's style to yours.... That you ... have imitated (as it were) this American seems to me to point to the existence of some real American mental quality."

Knowing how to twist the knife as only a sibling can, William intuited that of all Henry's American predecessors, Hawthorne was the one Henry was most in need of overcoming. Hawthorne represented a rootedness that James would always lack, a steeping in generations of history, an attachment to his place of birth as powerful as it was inevitable. Classifying Hawthorne as "an unqualified and unflinching American," James seeks in the biography he wrote for Macmillan's English Men of Letters series to define the limits of what that means for art, while prophesying the cosmopolitan alternative represented by his own career. The task of writing about Hawthorne was tortured. In an 1879 letter to a friend, the scholar Grace Norton, James confessed, "I have sent you a little biography of Hawthorne which I wrote, lately, sadly, against my will. I wanted to let him alone." It is a strange admission for many reasons, perhaps most importantly because so much of what James does say about the work and life of his most important forebear is uniquely insightful. Hawthorne could not have asked for a better reader than James, despite the latter's occasional condescension.

Yet James anticipated accurately the critical response to his book, which was widely viewed in its own time, and subsequently, as disrespectful. Though British reviewers generally approved, and E. L. Godkin commented that "it was the best thing of its kind that has appeared in this generation; and no [other] American living or dead could have written it," most American reviews were negative. "I thought they would protest over my calling New England life unfurnished but I didn't expect they would lose their heads at such a rate" James told the editor Thomas Perry. The biography is typically read as a rationale for why James moved to England, his apparent prerequisite for becoming a cosmopolitan writer. The main evidence for this rationale is the book's notorious list of the things absent from American life:

> [O]ne might enumerate the items of high civilisation, as it exists in other countries, which are absent from the texture of American life, until it should become a wonder to know what was left. No State, in the European sense of the word, and indeed barely a specific national name. No sovereign, no court, no personal loyalty, no aristocracy, no church, no clergy, no army, no diplomatic service, no country gentlemen, no palaces, no castles, nor manors, nor old country-houses, nor parsonages, nor thatched cottages, nor ivied ruins; no cathedrals, nor abbeys, nor little Norman churches, no great Universities, nor public schools—no Oxford, nor Eton, nor Harrow; no literature, no novels, no museums, no pictures, no political society, no sporting class—no Epsom nor Ascot! Some such list as that might be drawn up of the absent things in American life—especially in the American life of forty years ago, the effect of which, upon an English or a French imagination, would probably, as a general thing, be appalling.

So what did America, in James's view, *possess*? A powerful oral culture and a commitment to individuality—a result of the society's youthfulness and abundant opportunities. For writers such as Hawthorne, there was also a deep rootedness or sense of place. No matter the character or condition of one's ancestors, the joy or painfulness of their experience, the consciousness of continuity with those who came before was like a spell that had never been broken. James clearly envies this: "It is only in a country where newness and change and brevity of tenure are the common substance of life, that the fact of one's ancestors having lived for a hundred and seventy years in a single spot would become an element of one's morality." The "imaginative American" must "keep reverting to this circumstance . . . keep analyzing and cunningly considering it." Knowing literary material when he sees it, James registers here a longing for an artistically enabling aptitude that he will always lack. As T. S. Eliot observed, where Hawthorne had "a sense of the past," James had "a sense of the sense," a remark that should not be taken as pejorative in light of Eliot's characterization of James as "the most intelligent man of his generation."

James was keenly aware of the difference between his own sense of the past and Hawthorne's. Discussing *The Scarlet Letter*, he observes a collective cultural pride in "America having produced a novel that belonged to literature, and to the forefront of it. Something might at last be sent to Europe as exquisite in quality as anything that had been received, and the best of it was that it was absolutely American; it belonged to the soil, to the air; it came out of the very heart of New England." Approaching the novel prompts an authorial primal scene not unlike the fear and awe generated by his childhood encounter with William Holman Hunt's painting of the sacrificial goat in exile. James remembers how a National Gallery exhibition featuring "a pale handsome woman" with "a great crimson A [...] remained vividly imprinted on my mind; I had been made vaguely frightened and uneasy by it; and when, years afterwards, I first read the novel, I seemed to myself to have read it before, and to be familiar with its two strange heroines."

James's ability to appreciate the complex psychologies of young girls comes through in his recognition of "little Pearl" as a "heroine" comparable to her mother, Hester Prynne. But what stands out especially in the account of Hawthorne's greatest work is the view of how he transforms a "well-worn theme...the combination of the wife, the lover, and the husband," into a tale of great moral luminousness. As James recognizes, "No story of love was surely ever less a 'love story,'" zeroing in on the novel's preoccupation with the aftermath of adulterous, forbidden passion, and its moral consequences. The biography is full of gems, like the appraisal of Emerson "as a sort of spiritual sun-worshipper, [who] could have attached but a moderate value to Hawthorne's catlike faculty of seeing in the dark," or the description of Thoreau's "remarkable genius for the observation of the phenomena of woods and streams, of plants and trees, and beasts and fishes, and for flinging a kind of spiritual interest over these things."

The strongest evidence of homage is identification, and it is in places where what James says about Hawthorne seems most about himself that his admiration sparkles. Thus, the description of Hawthorne's peculiar brand of realism, which requires the reader to "look for his local and national qualities between the lines of his writing and in the *indirect* testimony of his tone, his accent, his temper, of his very omissions and suppressions." James sees Hawthorne's perspective on the Civil War, which defined his final years, as "an example of the way an imaginative man judges current events—trying to see the other side as well as his own, to feel what his adversary feels, and present his view of the case."

Though the "Custom-House Preface" that introduces *The Scarlet Letter* is viewed by many readers as obscure and off-putting, James pronounces it "the most perfect of all Hawthorne's compositions." James dwells on Hawthorne's occupation in the Custom House, referring repeatedly to the "official station" and "office" Hawthorne occupied just before writing *The Scarlet Letter*. In so doing, he plants a clue to one of the most important moments in *The Portrait of a Lady*, published two years after the Hawthorne book. James draws an implicit thread from Hawthorne's "emolument," courtesy of President Polk, the discovery of Hester's scarlet letter, and the "discovery" of Isabel Archer, the young heroine who is found in a similar "office" in Albany, by her expatriated aunt, Mrs. Touchett, and brought to England to meet her destiny. The imaginative infusion of Isabel's "office" with that of the Custom House links James's aesthetic to his struggle with the authorial example of Hawthorne, and finally to the ambitions of his first great heroine, whose origins, like Hawthorne's and his own, lie in the provincial world.

James's description of Isabel resonates with Hawthorne's portrait of life as a Custom House officer. In both cases, discovery arouses mystery—in Hawthorne, "how it was to be worn, or what rank, honor, and dignity, in by-past times, were signified by it, was a riddle"; in James, the "mysterious apartment...called, traditionally, no one knew why, the office. Whose office it had been and at what period it had flourished, she never learned." Like Isabel, James plans for his imagination to take flight far beyond the national boundaries that enclosed Hawthorne, but he would never forget the American roots that provided the foundation for who he was and who he could be.

Chapter 2
Global apprenticeship

By the mid-1870s it had become clear to James that England was the most hospitable country in which to launch a writing career. "I take very kindly indeed to London," he wrote to his mother in 1876, "I like feeling in the midst of the English world, however lost in it I may be. I find it interesting, inspiring, even exhilarating." And although his returns to America would be frequent, by 1881 he was assured that "My choice is the old world—my choice, my need, my life." He lamented that the burden of the American writer was greater than that of the European, for an American "*must* deal" with Europe, while no European writer is ever called upon to deal with America. But "as an artist and as a bachelor; as one who has the passion of observation and whose business is the study of human life," James "took possession of London," which he felt "to be the right place."

In keeping with his expatriation, James schooled himself deliberately in the methods of an international array of masters, including Honoré de Balzac, Charles Baudelaire, Émile Zola, George Eliot, Thomas Hardy, and Ivan Turgenev, among others. James famously advised the "novice" writer in "The Art of Fiction" to "try to be one of the people on whom nothing is lost," and the formidable reviews he produced in the 1870s and 1880s when he was pursuing a global apprenticeship shows him to have absorbed his own advice. James as reviewer is attentive to things we would expect: the business of writing; the relationship between life and work; violations of the author's privacy; the narrative donnée (its subject and intended technique); the author's preparatory research. Through what James admires and disparages in others we learn about the writer he aspired to be. While granting the French novelist Honoré de Balzac his genius, for instance, James bemoans the excessiveness of Balzac's literary worlds. The works lack clear principles of selectivity, as well as a discriminating moral sensibility.

Among the principles James articulated in reviews throughout his career was that if an author belongs to "the limited class of very careful writers," then the work itself is invested with any aspects of personality, values, and political views that a reader should need. While it is perhaps inevitable, he confesses in a review of his Russian mentor Ivan Turgenev, that there is "curiosity as to the private personality" of authors, it is best that a skillful reading of the work serve as a guide to such information. James's implication is that the deeper our engagement with what writers create, the greater our chances of finding the creator. Like D. H. Lawrence, who insisted in his brilliantly cryptic *Studies in Classic American Literature*, "never trust the artist, trust the tale," and the Czech writer Milan Kundera, who recommended that "novelists who are more intelligent than their books should go into another line," James believed that the minds and souls of great writers were located in the productions that made them worthy of attention in the first place.

Reviewing afforded James the opportunity to test fundamental assumptions like these, and also to examine issues and ideas that did not come naturally. Reading his reviews exposes his interest in things with which he is not readily identified, such as technology and innovation, the lives of the poor, scientific theories, and politics and government. Thus, in a review of histories by the father-son French writers the Ampères, we find James speculating on how different the world might have been had the electric telegraph been "invented in time to be used at the battle of Waterloo." More predictable is the way his cosmopolitanism inspires interest in national and cultural distinctions. The "fantastic cohesiveness" of Balzac's "Comedie Humaine" is an accomplishment "on the imaginative line" akin to "what Comte's 'Positive Philosophy' is on the scientific." Both "great enterprises are equally characteristic of the French passion for completeness," he declares, "a French brain alone could have persisted in making a system of all this." Yet who would have imagined Henry James a reader of Auguste Comte, the founder of sociology?

And who would have anticipated his fascination with the multivolume journals of the explorer David Livingstone, which James describes as "a pathless forest." A devout missionary inspired by a divine light, Livingstone traversed "an immense region, exploring the basin of the great Lualaba and Chambeze Rivers, and the three great lakes—Nyassa, Bangweolo, and Tanganyika—marching for weeks together through forest and jungle, and living for months in African villages." James is struck by the extreme contrast between the natural beauty Livingstone documents and the accounts of a slave trade so vicious that it causes "literal broken-heartedness," in victims who "drooped and pined" and eventually died. Yet James's empathy and enlightenment has limits, as confirmed by his recourse to stereotypes of the faithful versus devious African servant and brutal Arab slaver.

Reviewing a range of peers involves a continuous assessment of where his own work and ambitions fit. Here self-understanding proves keen. In a piece on the death of Turgenev from the 1880s that includes a description of their friendship, James confronts "why it was (and it interested me much), that my writings could not appeal to him. He cared, more than anything else, for the air of reality, and my reality was not to the purpose. I do not think my stories struck him as quite meat for men. The manner was more apparent than the matter; they were too *tarabiscote* [ornate, convoluted], as I once heard him say of the style of a book—had on the surface too many little flowers and knots of ribbon."

No writer could have been further from James's own literary instincts than Balzac, which is why his accounts of the French master are among the most revealing of his reviews. Balzac is, by James's description, a materialist:

> There is nothing in all imaginative literature that in the least resembles his mighty passion for *things*—for material objects, for furniture, upholstery, bricks and mortar. The world that contained these things filled his consciousness, and *being* at its intensest, meant simply being thoroughly at home among them...to get on in this world, to succeed, to live greatly in all one's sense, to have plenty of *things*—this was Balzac's infinite.... It was natural, therefore, that the life of mankind should seem to him above all an eager striving along this line.

James's admiration for Turgenev is founded in what distinguishes him from Balzac, who desired above all "to be the great showman of the human comedy," and writers like Charles Dickens, Sir Walter Scott, and George Sand, who care "almost supremely, for their fable, for its twists and turns and surprises, for the work they have in hand of amusing the reader." Turgenev, in contrast, is preoccupied with subject matter: "There is literally almost nothing he does not care for. Every class of society, every type of character, every degree of fortune, every phase of manners.... He has an eye for all our passions, and a deeply sympathetic sense of the wonderful complexity of our souls." James cites Turgenev's tales about a deaf and dumb serf and his lap dog, and about a religious fanatic, as examples of his moral vision and psychological acuity. Recalling his biography of Hawthorne, James commends the way Turgenev's "works savor strongly of his native soil, like those of all great novelists, and give one who has read them all a strong sense of having had a prolonged experience of Russia."

Yet Turgenev seems "a man disappointed...in the land that is dear to him," and James insists that though his gloom "has its element of error...it has also its element of wisdom. Life *is*, in fact, a battle." On this point, James suggests, optimists and pessimists agree: "Evil is insolent and strong; beauty enchanting but rare; goodness very apt to be weak; folly very apt to be defiant; wickedness to carry the day; imbeciles to be in great places, people of sense in small, and mankind generally, unhappy."

James finds a method for accommodating this fate in a different source, the works of Epictetus edited by the minister-author Thomas Wentworth Higginson. The philosophy of this "deformed and poor" Roman slave, writes James, affirms that "life is beset on every side with poverty and suffering.... Every man is subject, as a matter of course, to certain visitations of cruelty and injustice." Though "it is not in our power to be rich, to be free, to be sound of body...it is in our power to be resigned to poverty, slavery, and sickness. It is in our power to live philosophically; i.e. patiently, passively, in conscious accordance with the divine part of our nature." Ever the son of his father, James is suspicious of this stringent spirituality. "The Stoicism of Epictetus," he concludes, "is in its uncompromising sternness, its harshness, its one-sidedness, its lack of imagination, a thoroughly Roman principle." James admires, but from a great distance, "a religious instinct as pure as the devotion of a Christian saint."

Though James learned from European forebears, this was not at the expense of American and English ones. When it came to American women writers, whom he seemed to view as competitors with an unfair advantage, James could be downright grudging—even toward friends. An 1887 review of the work of Constance Fenimore Woolson opens with a complaint:

> Flooded as we have been in these later days with copious discussion
> as to the admission of women to various offices, colleges, functions,

and privileges, singularly little attention has been paid, by themselves at least, to the fact that in one highly important department of human affairs their cause is already gained....In America, in England, to-day, it is no longer a question of their admission into the world of literature: they are there in force....In America, at least, one feels tempted at moments to exclaim that they are in themselves the world of literature.

This seems to explain the review that follows, where Woolson's hikes in the southern terrain that provides the locale for much of her widely admired fiction become a sign of lonely depression; her interest in worlds that have escaped the attention of novelists becomes a feminine appetite for the picturesque; her focus on marriage indicates an avoidance of more "manly" concerns; and the label "conservative," with which he stamps her work, is one he would loathe to have applied to his own. James's biographer Lyndall Gordon characterizes the review as "a calculated betrayal," carrying "an armoury of stings in its velvet glove." The added sting was James's choice to publish the piece in *Harper's Weekly*, addressing his barbs to the heart of Woolson's readership.

Yet James's account of Woolson conveys a recognition of shared literary values; indeed, he could be harsher in reviewing writers with whom he felt at odds. He seems outraged, for instance, by Émile Zola's *Nana*: "On what authority does M. Zola represent nature to us as a combination of the cesspool and the house of prostitution? On what authority does he represent foulness rather than fairness as the sign that we are to know [Nana] by? On the authority of his predilections alone: and this is his great trouble and the weak point of his incontestably remarkable talent." Of Dickens he writes,

> We are convinced that it is one of the chief conditions of his genius not to see beneath the surface of things. If we might hazard a definition of his literary character, we should, accordingly, call him

the greatest of superficial novelists. We are aware that this definition confines him to an inferior rank in the department of letters which he adorns; but we accept this consequence of our proposition. It were, in our opinion, an offence against humanity to place Mr. Dickens among the greatest novelists.... He is master of but two alternatives: he reconciles us to what is commonplace, and he reconciles us to what is odd.

Thomas Hardy's novels also come in for rough treatment. "The author has little sense of proportion and almost none of composition" he writes of *Far from the Madding Crowd*, "Everything human in the book strikes us as factitious and insubstantial; the only things we believe in are the sheep and the dogs."

In Constance Fenimore Woolson, James appraises an author with similar values whose work he considers inferior, while Zola, Dickens, and Hardy he considers competitors with utterly remote styles and subjects. In George Eliot, James encountered an author whose work would deeply inform his own. Thus, it is no surprise that when James writes about Eliot, he can seem competitive, even petty. His review of *Middlemarch* asserts with bristling authority that it "is at once one of the strongest and one of the weakest of English novels.... Certainly the greatest minds have the defects of their qualities, and as George Eliot's mind is preeminently contemplative and analytic, nothing is more natural than that her manner should be discursive and expansive." While admitting that Dorothea Brooke is a genuine, even remarkable heroine, he argues that *Middlemarch* ought to have provided a weightier drama more worthy of her. Still, he ends with unstinting praise for "the constant presence of thought, of generalizing instinct, of *brain*, in a word, behind her observation, [that] give the latter its great value and her whole manner its high superiority." *Middlemarch* unquestionably "remains a very splendid performance...a contribution of the first importance to the rich imaginative department of our literature."

Just as Hawthorne and Eliot provide masterful characters and plots as precursors to Isabel Archer affronting her destiny, so too do James's own early heroines from this apprenticeship period. In Eugenia Münster, Daisy Miller, and Catherine Sloper, of, respectively, *The Europeans* (1878), *Daisy Miller* (1878), and *Washington Square* (1880), we find variations on fictional experience that seed the ground for James's achievement in *The Portrait of a Lady* (1881). Each of these heroines is a bold creation who provokes a quandary in her fictional society. By making complexly imagined young women the engines of these stories, these narratives show how riveting the question of what the young woman will do, and why, can be.

The Europeans is a comedy of manners, a seemingly slight novella about a (relatively) poor brother and sister who come to "the ancient city of Boston" to meet their wealthy uncle and cousins. The narrative recounts in classic comic terms the series of misunderstandings that follow from contrasting cultural norms and etiquette, before their resolution in a series of marriages. At the center of the work is the Baroness Münster, a thirty-three-year-old who has "married up" and has recently been asked by her husband, a German prince, Adolf of Silberstadt-Schreckenstein, to renounce their vows so that he may find a new bride with more financial and political capital. Baroness Münster therefore seeks an American opportunity to compensate her anticipated losses. The baroness is moody, opinionated, and accustomed to admiration, though she is described as "not pretty," but possessed of a face that was "most interesting and agreeable," and eyes that are "charming…brilliant, quickly glancing, gently resting, full of intelligence."

To her Boston kin, who are restrained and dutiful in a way that is part Puritan, part bourgeois, she is exotic and invests their lives with much-needed drama. Accompanying the baroness is her younger brother, Felix, a painter, as sunny and light as she is morbid and inscrutable. An enthusiast whose effortless charm exerts a magnetic force, especially on women, his disposition is the ideal complement to his sister's. The circle of the Boston cousins includes an inevitable minister, Mr. Brand, and a wealthy neighbor, Robert Acton, who has traveled the world, including China, and seems a viable suitor for the cosmopolitan baroness. Felix has his choice of prospective wives in his cousins, Charlotte and Gertrude Wentworth, though the latter, with whom he falls almost immediately in love, has been promised to the minister.

The novella opens on a graveyard viewed from "a gloomy-looking inn," reminding us that though the goal is entertainment, Hawthorne in general, and *The Scarlet Letter* (whose opening features a graveyard and prison) in particular, is never far from James's mind. *Daisy Miller*, James's first unqualified success, both critically and in terms of sales, is a different kind of work, focusing on an individual and her fate rather than on an ensemble representing a clash of cultures. The clash in this work is among Americans regulating their own in insular communities abroad, rather than between people from the Old World and the New. The novella's titular character is represented as a quintessential American girl of the era on a European tour with her mother and kid brother. In little more than fifty pages, James establishes a mystery—is Daisy Miller innocent or corrupt, independent or obtuse—staged through the perspective of a smitten young American, Frederick Winterbourne. Winterbourne is drawn first, predictably, to her looks, and then to the question of her moral condition.

The daughter of a Schenectady, New York, businessman who has made a fortune, and a listless mother who is clueless about social norms, Daisy is free to indulge her whims, a situation that, given her ignorance of etiquette and of elite customs everywhere, has precipitated her ostracism. When Winterbourne meets her, at the novella's start, she is already the subject of talk, and his own casual associations with her, which involve conducting her to a castle without chaperones, results in her further exclusion from "good" society. The novella explores the classic ethnographic conundrum that James will develop in subsequent fiction: Winterbourne is both a detached observer and a participant whose actions significantly impact the story's outcome. By enjoying her company in ways that invite social disapproval, and failing to protect her from those who spurn her, he, as much as anyone, affects Daisy's fate. Yet like many of James's male characters, early and late, he continues to view himself as largely disinterested.

Though much too young and unsophisticated to fend for herself, Daisy, with her undisciplined brother, Randolph (who subsists on candy and has no designated bedtime), is thrown to the wolves in the form of detached young men like Winterbourne, predatory Europeans eager to pursue a rich American girl, and the harsh judgments of American busybodies abroad. Socialized to regard herself as an object of admiration whose value can only be verified by male attention, yet unaware of the differences between appropriate and inappropriate beaux, Daisy is ruined by flirtations that result in her violation of social mores and ultimate death from Roman fever, contracted by going about at night with a questionable Italian named Giovanelli—"not a gentleman...only a clever imitation of one."

Daisy's fatal illness seems a punishing prophecy of what befalls American girls who violate established customs, whether from incomprehension or spite, and it was taken as such by readers of the time. One contemporary critic proclaimed that *Daisy Miller* succeeded in educating a generation of American girls, "who learned more from it than they would through a volume of well-intentioned maxims." William Dean Howells credited James's novella with having altogether eliminated this young female American type: "In 1870 you saw and heard her everywhere in the European continent; in 1880 you sought her in vain."

But the most important question raised by *Daisy Miller* is whether its heroine achieves tragic dimension. James liked the novella enough to revise it for the New York Edition of his work, and the persistent ambiguity of her portrait suggests a commitment to deepening a type usually dismissed as frivolous. Winterbourne's shifting attitude prompts sympathy for Daisy. Thus, Winterbourne "wondered how she felt about all the cold shoulders that were turned toward her, and sometimes it annoyed him to suspect that she did not feel at all." But "at other moments he believed that she carried about in her elegant and irresponsible little organism a defiant, passionate, perfectly observant consciousness of the impression she produced." References to her affect further reinforce sympathy: her repeated nervous laughter upon learning that she is shunned by Winterbourne's aunt ("she gave a little laugh," he "fancied there was a tremor in her voice"), and the final intimation that she welcomes death ("'I don't care,' said Daisy in a little strange tone, 'whether I have Roman fever or not!'"). The suggestion that she is wronged by those who dismiss her as a superficial flirt—members of the novella's fictional community, the novella's critics—endures beyond the ending. This is perhaps why Daisy, as much as any character James created, is memorable. And though she seems slight, consistent with the spare narrative that contains her, she manages to encompass a profound truth about young female vanity and the sensitivities and aspirations it camouflages. It is a truth that spoke to readers in James's time, and still speaks to them today.

Despite lacking beauty and talent, or perhaps because of it, the most intriguing of this trio of early James heroines is Catherine Sloper of *Washington Square*. She is a young woman distinguished by will, a resistance on the order of Melville's "Bartleby the Scrivener" to the domineering charismatic father to whom she is also somehow completely devoted. This is because Catherine's other outstanding quality is a capacity for unwavering love: first for her father, who is loyal to his daughter, though she has always disappointed him, and then for the narcissistic young man whose courtship is motivated by her inheritance. If love itself, the capacity to be stirred by passion for another, is enough to make a life meaningful, then hers is indeed so.

What makes *Washington Square* captivating is that the substantial heroine is provided a male counterpart of equal dramatic weight. Dr. Austin Sloper is introduced as an accomplished Manhattan physician, one whose "learning and skill were very evenly balanced...a scholarly doctor." At the same time, he is "a local celebrity...and he passed in the best society of New York for a man of the world." Suited to his vocation and favored by fortune, the doctor falls in love with an attractive heiress, marries, and seems destined for happiness, but then come two major losses: the death of a promising first-born son (whom he had hoped "to make an admirable man"), and the death of his wife shortly after the birth of his daughter, Catherine. "For a man whose trade was to keep people alive he had certainly done poorly in his own family." Still, the popular young doctor "escaped all criticism but his own.... He walked under the weight of this very private censure for the rest of his days, and bore forever the scars of a castigation to which the strongest hand he knew had treated him on the night that followed his wife's death."

This pivotal characterization of Dr. Sloper is often overlooked by critics who tend to focus on his apparent disdain for Catherine. Yet the novel is preoccupied with the nature of love, and the significance of the fact that the doctor is raising his daughter in the aftermath of great loss cannot be overestimated. Does the doctor reject his daughter *because* he has loved and paid the highest price? Is he *afraid* to love Catherine as he might? Or is his indifference a consequence of his hyper-criticalness and subsequent disappointment in the plain and stolid offspring who replaced the brilliant wife and son? And what of Catherine herself: as one who has never loved and lost, never known the mother who succumbed after childbirth, nor the brother dead at three, her gift for attachment provides an ongoing contrast to her father's remoteness.

The narrator intimates that one source of this remoteness is Dr. Sloper's distaste for women. Though "he was to a certain extent what is called a 'ladies' doctor,' his private opinion of the more complicated sex was not exalted. He regarded its complications as more curious than edifying and he had an idea of the beauty of *reason*, which was on the whole meagerly gratified by what he observed in his female patients." His wife was an exception to this rule, but his daughter, and his sister, Mrs. Penniman, who moves in to help care for the motherless girl, are not. And though his keenest hope for Catherine was that she be intelligent, she seems to occupy the middle rung in every way. The doctor "had moments of irritation at having produced a commonplace child," but "did his duty with exemplary zeal, and recognized that she was…faithful and affectionate."

It is precisely this mediocrity that makes the attention of Morris Townsend, the handsome young fortune hunter she meets at a party, so suspect. While the doctor is not opposed theoretically to a penniless partner (it is revealed that Townsend, having gone through his own small fortune, now sponges off his sister, a struggling widow with five children), he sincerely wishes that his daughter "might really be loved for her moral worth." A contest ensues between Dr. Sloper's sister, Mrs. Penniman, who defends Townsend's suit because she is taken by him and finds the situation romantic, and the doctor, who fears that his daughter is being seduced by an exploitative narcissist.

Catherine herself does what she does best: stirred by Townsend's attractiveness, she falls quickly in love while heeding her father's opposition to a marriage between them. Caught between her passion for this handsome young man whose appearance and interest are so unexpected, and her filial love, both of which are genuinely powerful, Catherine enters a state of paralysis, as a

Henry James

spectator on her own entrapment: "She watched herself as she would have watched another person, and wondered what she would do. It was as if this other person, who was herself and not herself, had suddenly sprung into being, inspiring her with a natural curiosity as to the performance of untested functions."

Her solution, which is a kind of marvel in its own right, is to do nothing, and hope that her father will relent, a reaction that can be seen as a form of stoicism. And indeed James emphasizes her faith: "Catherine expected a good deal of Heaven....Heaven would invent some way of reconciling all things—the dignity of her father's errors and the sweetness of her own confidence, the strict performance of her filial duties, and the enjoyment of Morris Townsend's affection." In realizing her destiny, Catherine anticipates the circumstances of both Isabel Archer and Pansy Osmond in *Portrait of a Lady*. The beginning of chapter 18 casts Catherine's potential defiance as a spiritual violation, on the order of Isabel's potential defiance of Osmond. Isabel, sitting by the fire, thinks, "He had expected his wife to feel with him and for him, to enter into his opinions, his ambitions, his preferences; and Isabel was obliged to confess that this was no great insolence on the part of a man so accomplished and a husband originally at least so tender. But there were certain things she could never take in." In *Washington Square*, "Catherine sat alone by the parlour fire—sat there more than an hour, lost in her meditations....She had an immense respect for her father, and she felt that to displease him would be a misdemeanor analogous to an act of profanity in a great temple." A subsequent encounter between Catherine and Dr. Sloper foreshadows scenes of Pansy's submission to Osmond: "Her father sat looking at her, and she was afraid he was going to break out into wrath; his eyes were so fine and cold. 'You are a dear faithful child,' he said at last. 'Come here to your father.' And he got up holding out his hands toward her. The words were a surprise and they gave her an exquisite joy."

Both Catherine and Pansy love young men forbidden by their fathers, and both remain loyal to those fathers. Still, *Washington*

Square has none of the sinister betrayals that predominate in *Portrait*. Dr. Sloper is intimidating, but he is a good man whose aversion to Morris Townsend is warranted and in his daughter's best interests. Nor does he ever stop trying to understand and appreciate her. And Catherine herself seems capable of a spiritual peace that transcends the suffering of Isabel Archer. This seems largely because *Washington Square* avoids the marriage that would make the young woman miserable. The paternal figure who prevents the heroine's marriage to the man she desires is compromised, but that doesn't make marriage a hopeful prospect for anyone. Every marriage depicted ends in loss and penury, and the novella stands as one of James's early trenchant critiques of the institution.

But even more, it is a rich psychological study of a phenomenally interesting young woman—interesting on her own terms, not in the terms of cultural convention. Catherine "became an admirable old maid. She formed habits, regulated her days upon a system of her own, interested herself in charitable institutions.... This life had, however, a secret history...that Morris Townsend had trifled with her affection, and that her father had broken its spring.... Nothing could ever undo the wrong or cure the pain that Morris Townsend had inflicted on her, and nothing could ever make her feel towards her father as she felt in her younger years."

This ending suggests that Catherine has been broken, but her final act discloses something altogether different: that through her loss of the faculties—love, loyalty—that have defined her being, she has achieved power. This is confirmed by her repudiation of Dr. Sloper's final request: that she promise never to marry Morris Townsend. Though Catherine knows that she will never do so, she recognizes the request itself as a violation of her independence and rejects it. This final act of dissent shows that she has learned to live for herself, a formidable achievement for a woman of her era.

Chapter 3
The James brand

More than any major writer of his era, James understood that a cosmopolitan sensibility was necessary to the modern literary vocation. As he put it in *Hawthorne*, the American writer of his day would be "more Europeanized" and more equipped to accommodate "the idiosyncrasies of foreign lands." The Civil War afforded national recognition "of the world being a more complicated place," and so "the good American in days to come will be a more critical person;" he will have "eaten of the tree of knowledge" and will be, "without discredit to his well-known capacity for action, an observer."

In making a case for the new cosmopolitanism of the American writer, James identified "moral consciousness," an "unprecedented spiritual lightness and vigor," as a distinctive national quality. During the period when he was introducing his brand to an Anglo-American public, James honed his signature subject: plotting the fates of Americans abroad. Protagonists such as Roderick Hudson (of *Roderick Hudson*, 1875), Christopher Newman (of *The American*, 1877), Daisy Miller, and Isabel Archer all suffer and learn in complex European domains that challenge their consciences.

If James was not the inventor of the international novel, he was certainly one of its most important proponents and developers.

The story of Americans going abroad to discover both the world and themselves is one that is permanently identified with him. Having traveled and lived abroad from a young age and then embraced the expatriate condition as an adult, he was singularly equipped to mine this genre. Yet despite his sense of himself as a cosmopolitan who bridged the old world with the new, he never failed to privilege an idealistic avidity for experience that he associated with his native land.

The international scene was not only a place for cultivating individuals, however. It could also be corrupting. And a striking and overlooked feature of James's novels, early to late, is how many of the morally discredited, downright villainous characters are American. The typical Jamesian "innocent" is surrounded by American expatriates who have lost their way, ethically speaking. Characters such as the Lights (*Roderick Hudson*) and Gilbert Osmond and Madame Merle (*The Portrait of a Lady*) have been in the Old World, it seems, too long for their own good. As Americans themselves, who understand their compatriots better than the European natives, these expatriate characters are uniquely threatening to the fledgling American protagonists of so many of James's fictions.

James's focus on those inhabiting the margins, like travelers and exiles, allowed him to explore the defining rites of different cultures. By representing England and Europe primarily through the perspectives of nonnatives, he was able to foreground the particularity and oddity of cultural traditions. In the worlds of James's fictions, where the mixing of cultures is constant, everyone is a stranger to someone, and therefore no habits or values are natural or inevitable. Moreover, transcending nationality was James's goal as an artist. He wrote in an 1888 letter to William, "I aspire to write in such a way that it would be impossible to an outsider to say whether I am at a given moment an American writing about England or an Englishman writing about America (dealing as I do with both countries), and so far as being ashamed of such an ambiguity I should be exceedingly proud of it."

While "the international theme" was his special contribution to the world of letters, James was also by the 1880s beginning to set out the principles of fictional form that would establish him as a master of literary craft. "The successful application of any art is a delightful spectacle, but the theory too is interesting," he observed in "The Art of Fiction" (1884), his first major venture in this vein, adding, "though there is a great deal of the latter without the former I suspect there has never been a genuine success that has not had a latent core of conviction." Effective art, he suggested, was the product of hard-won convictions. The more experienced the writer, the more capable he was of articulating them. His own writing about writing culminated in the series of prefaces he wrote for the New York Edition of his work between 1906 and 1908. They ensured that the James brand—the basis of his reputation in his own time and for posterity—would have both a thematic and a formal component.

The American, for which James earned $1,350 through serial publication in the *Atlantic Monthly* from June 1876 through May 1877, was begun in Paris, where he was living to test the Parisian literary scene and to assess more generally the relationship between American and French society. He assured his friend William Dean Howells, who had contracted for the serial, of his contentment in Paris. Here "one can arrange one's life…exactly as one pleases," and "there are facilities for every kind of habit and taste, and…everything is accepted and understood." But he also saw that he would remain "an eternal outsider." Decamping for England in November 1876, he finished the monthly installments there and published the novel version in Boston in 1877 and London in 1879.

The plot of *The American* centers on Christopher Newman, a wealthy American businessman who comes to Paris to experience pleasurable things—art, women, culture—after a life of hard work. At the Louvre he befriends a poor young painter, a copyist named Noémie Nioche, and her father, and is then introduced to a beautiful widow, Claire de Cintré, with whom he falls in love. Claire is a Bellegarde, and her elite family harbors both a secret murder and an obsession with guarding their honor against unworthy suitors.

James was acutely aware of the national constraints—especially provincialism—that impeded his aspiration to international recognition. Yet he was sympathetic to the American qualities of his businessman protagonist: pragmatism, ambition, and indifference to class distinctions. The trouble with Christopher Newman is that his threat to the complacent aristocratic societies he enters is largely unconscious. While James identified with his character's ambition to preserve his democratic principles in the Old World, he is consistently critical of Newman's lack of insight. Newman misses too much to undermine in any profound way the snobbery and classism of his European hosts. Indeed, the gaps in Newman's awareness pinpoint precisely the schooling James himself sought to acquire as an international writer. Only in-depth, systematic knowledge of the European world would allow Americans to challenge its pernicious social forms and politics. To this end, James undertook deliberate study of French social and political life. He wrote to his father in 1875, saying, "I find the political situation here very interesting and devour the newspapers. The great matter for the last fortnight has been the election of seventy-five life-members of the new Senate, by the Assembly.... The Left has carried the whole thing through with great skill and good sense, and there is a prospect of there being a very well composed Senate."

Newman is from the start a compromised figure luxuriating in the innocence James worked so hard to overcome. Though mature and experienced, with a substantial record of service in the Civil War and a fortune accrued in the American West, he is unapologetic in his ignorance of foreign customs and inability to judge the treasures of the Louvre, where the novel's opening is set. The narrator confesses early on that "it must be admitted rather nakedly, that Christopher Newman's sole aim in life had been to make money.... This idea completely filled his horizon and satisfied his imagination. Upon the uses of money, upon what one might do with a life into which one had succeeded in injecting the golden stream, he had up to his thirty-fifth year very scantily reflected. Life for him had been an open game and he had played for high stakes."

Newman's weakness is self-satisfaction and incuriosity about the treacherous French society that becomes the site for his pursuit of the finer things in life. He has little understanding of his hosts, of their traditions, or of their senses of familial obligation and commitment to the Catholic church. When the young widow Claire de Cintré renounces their engagement to join the austere order of Carmelite nuns, he is dumbfounded. Visiting the convent near the novel's end, "it was not a reality to him. It was too strange and too mocking to be real . . . with no context in his own experience . . . he could see nothing, no light came through the crevices . . . behind it there was darkness with nothing stirring." Newman's failing is lack of empathy, an inability to envision the unfamiliar.

Still, James is hardly forgiving of Claire's manipulative aristocratic relatives, who are at odds with the largely positive historical transformations he builds carefully into his narrative. This is reinforced by James's characterization of the novel's plot in the preface he wrote for the 1907 New York Edition of *The American*—a representative American "cruelly wronged" and made to "suffer at the hands of persons pretending to represent the highest possible civilization."

In an 1876 letter to the *New York Tribune* about the acquisition of a great art work by an American collector, James expressed his "acute satisfaction" in "seeing America stretch out her long arm and rake in, across the green cloth of the wide Atlantic, the highest prizes in the game of civilization." Christopher Newman is incapable of such an appropriation, but the fascination with the transfer of value from European to American hands continued to animate James's great novels. For James such value had a formal correlative: "the general privilege of the artist" pursuing his "creative passion," which is "to him the highest of human fortunes, the rarest boon of the gods."

In reviewing for the *New York Times* the Library of America's *Collected Criticism of Henry James* when it was published in 1985, Michiko Kakutani emphasized the high standards James set for literary criticism. The critic, according to James, was "the real helper of the artist, a torch-bearing outrider, the interpreter, the brother." James continues in terms that are revealing of his view of the intricate interdependence among artist, critic, and audience. The life of the critic "is heroic, for it is immensely vicarious. He has to understand for others.... He deals with life at second-hand as well as at first; that is, he deals with the experience of others, which he resolves into his own."

Kakutani praises James's devotion to the idea that the novel should represent life, and that its plot and characters be as organic as life itself. She commends his appreciation of such disparate talents as Dickens, Trollope, Howells, and Flaubert, and his resistance to imposing his own literary values on the work of others. That the publication of James's critical oeuvre was considered worthy of a review by one of the *Times*'s leading pundits demonstrates just how brightly James's critical torch burned more than a century after the publication of his first major essay on criticism, "The Art of Fiction."

Published in London in *Longman's Magazine* in 1884, "The Art of Fiction" was a response to Walter Besant's 1884 lecture at the Royal Institution titled "Fiction as One of the Fine Arts," a clarion call for a novel of "conscious moral purpose" that would be distinguished from more popular sentimental works. The principle for which James's essay is known, the obligation of the novel to "represent life," is articulated through an analogy with painting; he notes that "their inspiration is the same, their process...their success...as the picture is reality, so the novel is history." But their differences become especially pronounced in the area of instruction: where the painter can make his practices plain to disciples, because "the grammar of painting is so much more definite," the literary artist is obliged to confess "Ah, well, you must do it as you can."

It is telling that one of James's direct sallies against Besant has to do with a point he finds disturbingly snobbish. Besant recommends that "a writer whose friends and personal experiences belong to the lower middle-class should carefully avoid introducing his characters into society," to which James responds, the "remark about the lower middle-class writer and his knowing his place is perhaps rather chilling; but for the rest I should find it difficult to dissent from any of these recommendations."

While James insists that good novels are the products of writers who possess a strong sense of reality, he denies the existence of a single means for calling that sense into being. This is not only because reality is vast and varied, but also because the writer's experience is always unlimited and incomplete. The best writers possess sensibility on the order of a "huge spider-web of the finest silken threads suspended in the chamber of consciousness," and there is no bar to what they might glean from "the faintest hints of life." Thus, a young woman without firsthand knowledge of the military might have much to offer on the subject if she is "one upon whom nothing is lost."

He recalls an English novelist, "a woman of genius," who was complimented for her portrait of the lives of French Protestant

51

youth. She was asked how she knew so much about experiences so remote from her own. She attributed her insight to a single moment in Paris, a glimpse through "an open door where, in the household of a *pasteur*, some of the young Protestants were seated at a table round a finished meal." That was all she needed, James notes, "to guess the unseen from the seen, to trace the implication of things, to judge the whole piece by the pattern."

Among James's many principles in "The Art of Fiction," none is more central to his writing than the idea of the "donnée," that the artist must be granted his subject, his idea, and that criticism be applied only to what he makes of it. This is the basis of literary authority: respect for the artist requires that he be allowed freedom of choice. Still, by granting equal legitimacy to the taste of readers, he confers upon them a reciprocal authority. "Nothing," he writes, "will ever take the place of the good old fashion of 'liking' a work of art or not liking it: the most improved criticism will not abolish that primitive, that ultimate, test." He rejects Émile Zola's belief that there can be an objective standard of aesthetic judgment; "I am quite at a loss to imagine anything (at any rate in this matter of fiction) that people *ought* to like or to dislike."

James concludes "The Art of Fiction" with two principles: (1) the quality of the novel depends on "the quality of the mind of the producer.... No good novel will ever proceed from the superficial mind"; and (2) no other art form is more capacious than the novel. "The other arts, in comparison, appear confined and hampered ... But the only condition that I can think of attaching to the composition of the novel is ... that it be sincere. This freedom is a splendid privilege, and the first lesson of the young novelist is to learn to be worthy of it." If one were to devise a moral for James's first great novel on the international theme, *The Portrait of a Lady* (1881), one could do no better than James's appeal to the young novelist: "learn to be worthy of freedom."

The Portrait of a Lady is the story of Isabel Archer, an American girl without a dowry who is discovered in Albany, New York, by an aunt who has expatriated herself in marrying a wealthy American committed to England. The aunt brings Isabel to the family estate near London, where her husband is dying, and Isabel promptly inspires the adoration of two eligible men: her cousin Ralph Touchett and his friend Lord Warburton. Isabel has already secured the devotion of an American, Caspar Goodwood, so Ralph and Warburton become additions to her bevy of conquests. Ralph, who is himself ailing, knows he can't *have* Isabel, so, hoping to liberate her from material concerns, requests of his father on his deathbed that he give Isabel a generous inheritance. The inadvertent result is that she becomes vulnerable to opportunists, specifically Madame Merle (an old friend of Isabel's aunt) and Gilbert Osmond, who scheme to make her fall in love with Osmond.

The first of James's international novels focused on the mind of a woman, *Portrait* reveals it to be an ideal register for the deep psychological transformations that became his trademark. For the originality and complexity of its characterizations and plot, its narrative beauty, and its engagement with literary forebears (in particular, Hawthorne's *The Scarlet Letter* and Eliot's *Middlemarch*), *Portrait* ranks with the great novels of the nineteenth century. James's self-conscious melding of form and content is forecast by the title: "the portrait" or artist's presentation of his subject will be as critical as the "lady" herself. Significantly, "*the*" aesthetic process is unique, whereas the lady is multiple, "*a*" representative American girl in Europe.

Throughout the novel, the American girl is viewed as an art object by everyone, including the girl herself. "She was better worth looking at than most works of art," Isabel's cousin Ralph Touchett reflects while showing her his art collection at the family's Gardencourt estate. Aesthetic power is a commodity in *Portrait* controlled above all by the narrating artist, but shared in turn by all the characters who seek to impose their imaginative designs upon each other. Isabel Archer falls for Gilbert Osmond in part because he seems to possess an exquisite aesthetic sensibility. The fact that Osmond's aestheticism is combined with moral corruption does not minimize how much Osmond has in common with Isabel's beloved and beneficent cousin Ralph. By investing Isabel with a fortune so that she might "meet the requirements of her imagination," Ralph is arguably more responsible than anyone for her sorry fate. As the critic R. P. Blackmur puts it, "Everyone tampers with Isabel, and it is hard to say whether her cousin, who arranges the bequest, or Osmond, who marries her because of it, tampers the more deeply."

And yet Isabel walks straight into the trap set by Gilbert Osmond and his lover, the sinister and seductive Serena Merle. Given the novel's focus on freedom and a young woman provided unlimited means to realize it, ultimate responsibility must lie with the subject herself. "If ever a girl was a free agent, she had been," Isabel concedes. As in *The Scarlet Letter*, among the critical questions raised by the novel is the author's attitude toward the woman blessed with looks, intelligence, idealism, and independence.

While the overall tone seems reverential, there are constant reminders of Isabel's limitations, as if her every advantage demands a qualification. Thus, males "were afraid of her," believing "that some special preparation was required for talking with her," given "her reputation of reading a great deal." But this is undermined forthwith: "She had a great desire for knowledge, but she really preferred almost any source of information to the printed page." A European sojourn where she will acquire what she has failed to obtain from books becomes therefore essential.

Yet the narrator also prepares us for her inability to learn from experience. "Her errors and delusions were such as a biographer interested in preserving the dignity of his subject must shrink from specifying. Her thoughts were a tangle of vague outlines which had never been corrected by the judgement of people speaking with authority. In matters of opinion she had had her own way, and it had led her into a thousand ridiculous zigzags....The girl had a certain nobleness of imagination which rendered her a good many services and played her a great many tricks."

Such passages suggest that Ralph's experiment is misguided from the start, based as it is on unqualified admiration for his legatee. The novel's fairy tale plot shows what happens to a woman who turns down two princes, one British and one American, to marry a frog, who only becomes more frog-like. While this could make *Portrait* a study of feminine agency gone wrong—give a woman freedom and she blows it—the deeper moral is that suffering is inevitable. And continuous suggestions of her profound desire to check her own freedom accentuate a human tendency to rush headlong into the very circumstances that will restrict and even afflict us.

Not that the novel minimizes how much Isabel's decision to marry Osmond is the result of her deception by Osmond as well as by Madame Merle. Persuaded of Osmond's nobility, she believes that her bequest is the proper due of a man whom she considers, like the discarded furniture in the Albany office, a "victim" of "injustice." Indeed, what she achieves with this endowment is different from "the enjoyment she found in the exercise of her power" following her refusal of Lord Warburton, the handsome British aristocrat, and Caspar Goodwood, the successful American entrepreneur. Like Dorothea Brooke in *Middlemarch*, another intellectually eager young woman dazzled by an apparently superior male mind that turns out to be stultifying, Isabel chooses a man she believes will help her develop.

Moreover, in marrying Osmond she assumes a power comparable to Ralph's: meddling with the destiny of another human being, which in James's worlds is the lone prerogative of the imaginative artist. However idealistic, these hubristic acts—Ralph's bequest to Isabel, and Isabel's transfer of that bequest to Osmond—can only produce suffering. Yet because suffering is the means to knowledge, the goal of all of James's characters, these acts are ultimately affirmed.

Toward the end of their tour of Ralph's art collection at Gardencourt just after they have met, Isabel announces, "Now I know more than I did when I began." Darkness has fallen and Ralph and Isabel are looking by candlelight. "You apparently have a great passion for knowledge," he says. Isabel's response seems digressive but is truly prescient: does the house have "a ghost?," to which Ralph answers, "I might show it to you, but you'd never see it. The privilege isn't given to everyone.... It has never been seen by a young, happy, innocent person like you. You must have suffered first, have suffered greatly, have gained some miserable knowledge. In that way your eyes are opened to it."

This dialogue is recalled in the novel's final chapter: "He had told her, the first evening she ever spent at Gardencourt, that if she should live to suffer enough she might someday see the ghost with which the old house was duly provided. She apparently had fulfilled the necessary condition; for the next morning, in the cold, faint dawn, she knew that a spirit was standing by her bed.... She stared a moment; she saw his white face—his kind eyes; then she saw there was nothing. She was not afraid; she was only sure."

Isabel sees the ghost not only because of her suffering, but because aboard the train from Rome to Ralph's deathbed she has come to terms with her mistakes and found peace: "There was nothing to regret now, that was all over. Not only the time of her folly, but the time of her repentance was far.... Deep in her soul—deeper than any appetite for renunciation—was the sense that life would be her business for a long time to come." Isabel's experience confirms a Jamesian ethic: pain is essential to human growth, and the more insight one derives from it, the more growth there is. Moreover, as Isabel tells Ralph before he dies, pain is "not the deepest thing; there's something deeper."

The something deeper is the existence of people to whom one feels obligated and the strength to fulfill those obligations. Isabel struggles with the decision to visit Ralph one last time because it requires she disregard Osmond's cruel opposition to her journey. By the end of *Portrait*, however, Isabel has discovered a "very straight path," triumphant in recognition of her obligation to Pansy, the vulnerable daughter of Osmond and Madame Merle, whom she loves.

In the preface to *The Portrait of a Lady* (1908) written for the New York Edition, James expressed satisfaction with the work's structural integrity, pronouncing it "the most proportioned of his productions after *The Ambassadors*," and marveling at the complexity of his protagonist and how he seemed "to have waked up one morning in possession" of the grand array of characters to complete "Isabel Archer's history." James's architectural metaphor extends to the preface's view of character as the foundation of story, calling it "the single small cornerstone ... for the large building of 'The Portrait of a Lady.'"

But the most memorable moment in this preface is the extended account of "the house of fiction." It has

> not one window, but a million—a number of possible windows not to be reckoned ... These apertures, of dissimilar shape and size, hang so, all together, over the human scene that we might have expected of them a greater sameness of report than we find. ... At each of them stands a figure with a pair of eyes, or at least with a field-glass, which forms, again and again, for observation, a unique instrument, insuring to the person making use of it an impression distinct from every other. He and his neighbors are watching the same show, but one seeing more where the other sees less, one

seeing black where the other sees white, one seeing big where the
other sees small, one seeing coarse where the other sees fine....
There is fortunately no saying on what, for the particular pair of
eyes, the window may *not* open...Tell me what the artist is, and
I will tell you of what he has *been* conscious. Thereby I shall express
to you at once his boundless freedom and his "moral" reference.

Morality comes from a breadth of perspective: the fuller the
artist's awareness, the more likely they will have the humanity and
intelligence to create great fiction. What defines the artist in
James's view is the capacity for endless curiosity. But while this
moral prospect depends on the artist, it is equally dependent on
something inherent in fictional form: the novel's openness, its
susceptibility to many different kinds of consciousness, becomes
an openness to many kinds of experience and by extension to
many kinds of human beings. This makes the novel a moral form
in its own right. What James is advancing here is a theory of the
novel's heterogeneity, which might even be thought of as an idea
of the novel's multiculturalism.

Thus, cultural and formal openness are here viewed as
interdependent, the novel's vast structural resources supporting a
hospitality to the varieties of human experience. No writer of the
time or since has written with more deliberation and
thoroughness about the possibilities of fiction as a craft. This is
undoubtedly one reason why James influenced such a diverse
array of writers in the twentieth century, and to this day. Among
those who have declared themselves protégés of the Master are
Virginia Woolf and James Baldwin, Dashiell Hammett and Philip
Roth, James Joyce, Toni Morrison and Julian Barnes.

The eighteen prefaces James wrote for the New York Edition
amount to a primer on literary method: the importance of point of
view and establishing the novel's central consciousness; the
attention to narrative design and the building blocks of plot; the
organic integrity of the work, which has its own inevitable size and

shape sometimes independent of the author's expectation; the congruence between rereading and rewriting ("the 'revised' element in the present Edition is…these rigid conditions of re-perusal, registered"). James embarked on the project of writing his prefaces with great ambition. His main purpose was to devise a method and theory of fiction using his own vast experience as a writer and applying his considerable critical skills to his own work. The project was at once distanced, an objective investigation of his best fiction, and intimate, a recollection of his subjective state while writing the different works.

Without liking James, without ever having read him, legions of aspiring writers in the twentieth and twenty-first centuries have internalized these legendary methods. They are the sine qua non of the extraordinary expansion of academic creative writing programs in the post–World War II era. The impact of the prefaces on the practice of writing, and on writers themselves, in the modern era cannot be overestimated. This is in no small part because the prefaces present novelistic practice as the most significant of human endeavors.

In his introduction to one of many reissues of *The Art of the Novel: Critical Prefaces*, the author Colm Tóibín states, "The prefaces are examples of thinking itself as something sensuous and fine, demanding and rewarding; they offer brilliant, sparkling insights into what fiction does and how it should be written and read. James saw the novel as something constructed, something willed into being by careful planning and arranging. But the art of fiction for him was not something dry and arid, or even pure. For him, the novel dramatized life itself, life at its richest and most unpredictable."

The theoretical rigor of James's fictional project explains why his oeuvre received so much attention from academic literary critics in the twentieth century, a critical industry that shows no signs of abating in the twenty-first. Critics of every political persuasion, armed with a variety of methods, have found James's works hospitable. For Marxists there is *The Princess Cassamassima*; for feminist and queer theorists, *The Bostonians*; for Foucauldians, *In the Cage* and *The Sacred Fount*; for psychoanalysts, *The Turn of the Screw*; and for postcolonial theorists, *The Golden Bowl*. Formalists, phenomenologists, and deconstructionists have found many James texts susceptible to treatment, feasting on their elaborately conceived designs.

Despite his passion for complexity, James never lost sight of the true object of writing: touching readers. James's response to the rise of a mass readership was vigilant but hopeful. He recognized that a reading audience composed of "the million," or even "the fast-arriving billion," will be a reading audience transformed. And what such an audience yields is "a wide picture of opportunities"—opportunities artistic and moral, and some of them unforeseeable. Finally, the object of any author worthy of substantial audiences was to create the reader required by his work. In the 1880s, James's effort toward this end had only just begun.

Chapter 4
Professional author

Between the late 1880s and the turn of the century, James published some of the most renowned works of his career. The volume and quality of novels and stories that he produced in this period made his name as a leading Anglo-American author. An aspect of James's professionalism that is sometimes missed is his aspiration to vast readerships; the fact that his books seldom sold widely came as a great disappointment and spurred his unsuccessful effort to reach a theater-going audience. Though he was able to support himself on his writings, he worried about money all of his adult life. Still, James's conviction that he was making an important contribution to Anglo-American culture never waned, nor did his steady focus on his signature subjects: coming of age, the traffic in women and capitalist exchange, the ties between primitive and modern civilizations, the relativist challenge to moral absolutes, the rise of mass culture and the role of art within it, and the nature of sexuality and desire.

James's mature fiction introduced a unique style into the literary canon. There had never been a literary voice like his, and there was no mistaking his narratives for others. This made him an occasional target of ridicule. For example, his brother William noted, "For gleams and innuendos and felicitous verbal insinuations you are unapproachable, but the *core* of literature is solid." One reader boasted of her ability to read James "in the original." And another recommended he not "put the tail of his sentences where the head belongs and the head where the body should be or the body where one naturally expects to see the tail."

Yet sympathetic readers grasped his purposes: how the style arose from keen theoretical interest in observation, and the power accorded human consciousness. For James, perceptions and thoughts were preeminent, so too emotions, which he privileged as the basis for his psychological realism. The principal actions of his plots were seeing, thinking, and feeling. As the American philosopher John Dewey observed, James was "concerned with the special and peculiar coloring that the mental life takes on in different individualities."

The distinctiveness of James's work did not limit its range and variety. As an ambitious writer, he sought to contribute significantly to multiple genres of the novel form, including satire (*The Bostonians*, 1886); ghost story (*The Turn of the Screw*, 1898); and dialogue novel (*The Awkward Age*, 1899). And through works like "The Aspern Papers" (1888), "The Altar of the Dead" (1895), "In the Cage" (1895), and "The Beast in the Jungle" (1903), he did more to develop what he called "the beautiful and blessed nouvelle," the short novel or long tale, than any writer of his time or since.

Equally noteworthy are his innovative methods and ideas; in James's oeuvre there are many firsts, and the courage it took to pursue subjects like those of *The Bostonians* should not be underestimated. Olive Chancellor is the first fully developed lesbian protagonist in fiction, and the novel as a whole explores lesbianism with an incomparable depth for the time. Given James's identification with decorum and his reticence about his own sexual proclivities, his determination to examine the subject with honesty and empathy is commendable.

The Bostonians is the only long novel by James set exclusively in America, with scenes primarily in Boston, Cambridge, and Cape

Cod. The novel's protagonists are Basil Ransom, a conservative lawyer from Mississippi, his cousin, Olive Chancellor, a Boston feminist, and Verena Tarrant, the offspring of a quirky bohemian family (her father is a mesmerist), who has been recruited as a spokesperson by the feminist movement. The cast of characters, filled out by an array of social reformers and journalists, includes Miss Birdseye, a grand dame revered as a pioneer by fellow feminists, whom contemporary critics took to be a denigrating caricature of Nathaniel Hawthorne's sister-in-law, Elizabeth Peabody. A reviewer in the *Atlantic Monthly* complained that "most of the characters are repellant," and asked if James "does not love them, why should he ask more of us?"

The Bostonians has long been an oddity in James's novelistic canon. While twenty-first-century audiences may find its approach to gender and sexuality surprisingly contemporary, critics have considered it less "Jamesian" than *The Portrait of a Lady* in tone and characterizations. *The Bostonians* is sometimes billed as the James novel for those who don't like James, a light work of conventional realism with melodramatic touches that James himself doubted (hence its omission from the New York Edition).

For those who view *Portrait* as an anti-marriage novel that dramatizes the need for feminist consciousness-raising, *The Bostonians* can seem a logical outgrowth of *Portrait*'s sorry account of a girl's "free agency." Others emphasize the novel's steeping in the rhetoric and themes of the American Civil War, noting the allegorical dimensions of the Union loyalist Olive Chancellor battling the Confederate veteran Basil Ransom for possession of "the American Girl" Verena Tarrant.

For some who admire it, *The Bostonians* displays patent historical engagements where much of James does not. It is a novel about Reconstruction and the social developments that defined this era: changing gender roles and ideas about sexuality; the rise of consumerism, advertising, and celebrity; the ongoing tension between the democratic values embodied by Verena Tarrant as the "vox populi" and class stratification.

James is alert to the ways in which class differences complicate changing attitudes toward gender, and his representation of the divide between social elites and the masses extends to transportation (upper-class carriages, working-class streetcars, penniless pedestrians). Features of an emerging multiculturalism are also evident, as when dilettantish upper-class New Yorkers are described as learning "some Talmud from Professor Gougenheim [*sic*]," signaling the assimilation of Jews in measured, intellectualized doses.

The novel is prescient in its portrait of the limitations and even destructiveness of traditional ideas of "men" and "women." However one interprets its gender politics, *The Bostonians* is a major American novel that takes the feminist movement seriously and portrays lesbian sexuality with real sensitivity. In describing the work-in-progress, James stressed these elements: it would expose the "invasions of privacy" in American society, while touching upon "the most salient and peculiar point in our social life, the situation of women, the decline of the sentiment of sex, the agitation in their behalf." Above all, it "should be a study of one of those friendships between women which are so common in New England." James might have been drawing here on any number of examples he knew, including the writers Annie Fields and Sarah Orne Jewett, or, closer to home, his sister, Alice, and her companion, the educator Katharine Peabody Loring.

The Bostonians opens with Olive Chancellor, the lesbian Northerner, exerting control over Basil Ransom, the heterosexual Southerner, by making him wait. They will soon be engaged in a more intense struggle over possession of the working-class girl, Verena Tarrant. Verena is beautiful and talented but naïve, which makes her susceptible to commodification. "There's money for someone in that girl," says the opportunistic "reporter, interviewer, manager, agent," Matthias Pardon, a prophecy soon realized by her father's decision to send Verena to live with Olive for a fee.

The novel's protagonists are compromised idealists. Olive is a guilt-ridden bourgeois who preys on the underclass, driven by a "desire to know intimately some *very* poor girl." Basil Ransom is a mediocre lawyer whose aspiration—"to make a living by his opinions"—is thwarted by the regular rejection of his submissions to conservative magazines. Seething with resentment about the South's defeat and the direction of society, he adopts a martial masculinity. His "rescue" of Verena from Olive's clutches and a feminist speaking tour is analogized to the stalking of Lincoln by John Wilkes Booth. Olive is similarly aggrandized as "some feminine firebrand of Paris revolutions…or even the sacrificial figure of Hypatia."

It is Verena's fate, of course, that is at issue here, and she is denied a say in her future, as the novel's inauspicious ending—her "tears… were not the last she was destined to shed"—makes clear. Verena is a victim of ideology, both conservative and radical. Her capacity to empathize with Basil's idealization of family values, as well as with Olive's feminist utopia, reveals her superiority to both of them. In this, she is akin to the author, and the ambivalence at the heart of *The Bostonians* may explain its poor reception. It was serialized in 1884–1885 in *Century Magazine*, whose editors reported little appetite for the thirteen installments, and the subsequent novel fared just as badly. Even those who found the portrait of American types brilliant were put off by its subject and tone.

Disappointing sales do not diminish the novel's breakthroughs, which were considerable. But by the 1890s James was confronting the painful reality that his serial and book sales were modest and his finances needed bolstering. In 1891 he confided to Robert Louis Stevenson, "Chastening necessity has laid its brutal hand on me and I have to try to make somehow or other the money I don't make by literature. My books don't sell, and it looks as if my plays might."

This turned out to be a vain hope. "I mean to wage this war ferociously for one year more," he wrote William in December 1893 of his efforts in the drama field, and then "'chuck' the whole intolerable experiment." A little over a year later, on January 5, 1895, the dismal premiere of James's play *Guy Domville*, featuring a popular actor, George Alexander, pushed him over the edge. While fellow writers in attendance—George Bernard Shaw, H. G. Wells, and Arnold Bennett—admired what they saw, James was booed by the larger audience, and he took this as the traumatic end to a cursed theatrical sojourn.

The Turn of the Screw was James's first major work following this defeat, its germ recorded in a journal entry of January 12, 1895. The bare outlines of the story—originally told by the archbishop of Canterbury to James at tea—are strikingly close to the actual plot of the novel: an isolated country house, sister and brother orphans left to the care of depraved servants who transfer their corruption to the children. The servants die, returning as ghosts that haunt the house and taunt the children to come "over to where they are" in their evil afterlife.

The germ remained undeveloped until James was approached in 1897 by Robert J. Collier, the editor of *Collier's Weekly*, who wanted a ghost story by a writer not known for producing them and acquisitioned a twelve-part serial. The genre, which virtually guaranteed a wide readership, turned out to be an ideal transition from *Guy Domville*. James had already written stories in this vein, and the supernatural was a familial preoccupation; Henry James Sr. was fascinated by spiritualism and spirit possession, and William did research on occult phenomena.

Like many contemporary intellectuals, William and Henry took ghosts seriously. They were friendly with Frederic W. H. Myers, who headed the Society for Psychical Research, and Henry was recorded in the minutes of a society meeting in London reading a report on behalf of his absent brother about a female medium who was occasionally overtaken by the spirit of a dead man. Society researchers sought positivistic evidence of ghosts and provided a steady stream of testimonies for public consumption. These accounts of specter sightings, which numbered in the thousands, were in turn avidly consumed by readers, who couldn't get enough of them.

The James brothers' views on ghosts were rooted in contemporary science, and also in their personal convictions about the fate of consciousness after death. Having enjoyed such fertile minds, and interacted with so many others, neither could accept that these vital organs would simply expire with the body. As William wrote in a letter to the Harvard professor Charles Eliot Norton, "I am as convinced as I can be of anything that this experience of ours is only part of the experience that is, and with which it has something to do; but *what* or *where* the other parts are, I cannot guess." In the essay "Is There a Life after Death?," Henry concurs, suggesting that preparation for an imaginatively heightened afterlife is made through long cultivation of the intellect. Death as Henry sees it is a release of the most advanced minds into an elite republic of consciousness. Liberated from cumbersome materiality, the mind can range freely. Moreover, it is in death, James holds, where we are known solely through the memories of others, that we have the most power to arouse love and to control loved ones.

Such assumptions inform the plot of *The Turn of the Screw*, which is concerned with the influence of the living by the dead. As the narrator, the governess transfixes her audience with her story from the beyond, and the divide between the dead and the living remains permeable throughout. The novel foregrounds boundaries of all kinds—architectural (doors, windows, corridors, stairways), natural (dawn, twilight), class (uncle/governess, servants/children, governess/housekeeper)—and their regular violation. It is the very function of ghosts to undermine confidence—for good or ill—that the dead are truly set apart.

The question that confronts every reader of the novel is whether the ghosts of Miss Jessel, the governess, and Peter Quint, the gardener, are "real" or figments of the current governess's imagination. Critics have quarreled since the work's publication about the authenticity of the ghosts. Some believe in them wholeheartedly, while others deem them hallucinations of an hysterical governess. What remains critical is James's own insistence on ambiguity; refusing to take an absolute stand on the issue, he understands, makes for a better story.

The reality or unreality of the ghosts is further complicated by the multiple frames. The novel's events are recounted by an unidentified narrator, who has heard them from a character named Douglas, who read them in a manuscript written by the governess; her first-person narrative enables her to speak from the grave.

A parson's daughter, hired by a wealthy guardian to tutor his charges, an eight-year-old niece and ten-year-old nephew at Bly, a remote country estate, the governess is instructed that she "should never trouble him—but never, never: neither appeal nor complain nor write about anything." For this, the guardian, "a lone man without the right sort of experience or a grain of patience," pays her a salary that so "much exceeded her modest measure" she cannot refuse.

What at first seems a pastoral utopia, however, soon becomes a nightmare, as the governess is subjected to visitations from the ghosts of Miss Jessel and Peter Quint, and then to increasingly desperate worry over the moral condition of the children. Do Miles and Flora know instinctively what the sexually transgressive governess and gardener seem to have modeled for them?

While *The Turn of the Screw* is more interested in the ontology of evil than in Calvinist notions of original sin, no reader can be secure about the children's essential innocence. As in *The Awkward Age*, the emphasis on how adult characters, and society at large, handle the precocious awareness of children leaves the question of the children's own sexual understanding entirely open.

The fundamental quandary persists: Are the children innocent, and what can innocence mean in the story's terms? And if the children have learned more than they should about adult sexuality, who is most responsible for it? The sinister Peter Quint, or the narrator whose passion can seem unbounded? The key to all this intrigue is the Freudian puzzle, which James anticipated, of what children know and when they know it. This is central to James's fiction of the 1890s, which repeatedly stages the experiences of children who are at once preternaturally perceptive about the adult world that surrounds them, while retaining an openness and naivete. Yet their complicated blend of attributes are not unlike those of adult protagonists in *The Ambassadors* and *The Golden Bowl*. For characters such as Lambert Strether and Maggie Verver must also undergo painful transitions from gullibility and trust to mature awareness.

As the ultimate example of James's portraits of innocents from the 1890s, *The Awkward Age* (1899) concerns an emergent female sexuality that prompts elaborate forms of vigilance. Female adolescents are, on the one hand, innocents whose entry into society requires the purification of cultural habits. But, on the other hand, over the novel's course, the female adolescent is increasingly viewed as herself a threat to social mores. Every attempt to preserve female innocence fails, and the failure is attributed to feminine nature rather than to society itself.

In his preface to the novel, James recalls his intent to explore a typical rite of passage, the introduction of female adolescents into the "liberal firesides" of modern England. "The account to be taken, in a circle of free talk, of a new and innocent, a wholly un-acclimatized presence," seems to James a subject "as limited as it was lively." The novel's cast includes Edward Brookenham, the passive cynical husband of Fernanda Brookenham ("Mrs. Brook"), who runs a closed salon where everything is permissible; their over-educated son, Harold; their eighteen-year-old daughter, Nanda; the wealthy Duchess, who pretends to represent established customs but is competing against Mrs. Brook to obtain the wealthiest possible husband for her niece, Aggie, the other eligible adolescent; the kind-hearted Mitchy who is fabulously rich and decidedly homely; Vanderbank, the civil servant, who has looks but no money; and Mr. Longdon, a representative of tradition, and a devotee of Nanda's grandmother, whom she, strikingly, resembles.

The crisis faced by the circle that frequents the Brookenham parlor is how to integrate their daughter, Nanda, without ruining her with their scandalous talk. How can her innocence be preserved while affording her the visibility that facilitates marriage and motherhood? These questions are further complicated by the fact that Mrs. Brook and Nanda are in love with the same man: the dazzling bachelor Vanderbank, who appears bent on remaining one. The novel concludes with Nanda's departure for a country estate, the ward of Mr. Longdon, a man three times her age; Aggie, newly married to Mitchy (the Duchess wins) but engaged in adultery with Penderton, a debauched aristocrat; and the other circle marriages floundering. With few prospects for generational continuity, English society as envisioned here has lost the ability to transmit inherited traits and values.

As victims and catalysts of this social sterility, the adolescent protagonists, Nanda and Aggie, have had antithetical educations. Aggie, a product of the Duchess's Old World constraints, is so ignorant she behaves as one "to whom the language of her companions was unknown." Nanda's upbringing, in contrast, is so open that she is apprised of the logic behind it. "Mother wants me to do everything," Nanda announces, she "is throwing me into the world." Whether Mrs. Brook's liberated childrearing practices express her contempt for prevailing norms or contempt for her daughter goes unanswered. By making Nanda dangerously knowledgeable, and therefore unmarriageable, Mrs. Brook undermines the interests of her class as well as Nanda's prospective happiness through marriage to Vanderbank.

Yet Vanderbank himself rejects the continuous overtures of Longdon, who presses his union with Nanda. Their climactic dialogue where Vanderbank makes his reluctance plain suggests that he is a closeted homosexual. Throughout this scene, the 1895 trial of Oscar Wilde, where he was convicted of "gross indecency" for homosexual acts, is recalled implicitly. Self-characterized as "a mass of corruption," Vanderbank is compared to "some prepossessing criminal who, in court, should have changed places with the judge." Remarking "how awfully" Longdon wants the marriage, Vanderbank receives, in the form of Longdon's retort, a veritable slap in the face: "How awfully *you* don't."

The legalistic rhetoric in this scene underscores Vanderbank's personal dilemma: his genuine respect for tradition and his displeasure over the degraded state of group morals puts him at war with his own erotic needs. In this way, he and Nanda are very much alike: united in their self-contempt. Nanda's fate is to love Vanderbank, to whom she is "precisely obnoxious," while Vanderbank's fate is the renunciation of an outlawed desire.

Vanderbank's embattled sexuality is at one with the dysfunction of marriage and mothering in *The Awkward Age*. In the novel, individual suffering corresponds to problems of a national, even global scale. James's ingenious coupling of generational conflict with larger fears about the British Empire's decline enables the exploration of moments of transition in social-psychological as well as political terms. The anxieties aroused by rites of passage affect individuals who become lenses for focusing wider transformations.

To this end, James employs a new technique he will test again in *The Golden Bowl*: designating a principal character for each of *The Awkward Age*'s ten books. "In sketching my project," James recalls in his 1908 preface, "I drew on a sheet of paper—and possibly with an effect of the cabalistic...the neat figure of a circle consisting of a number of small rounds disposed at equal distance about a central object. The central object was my situation, my subject in itself, to which the thing would owe its title, and the small rounds represented so many distinct lamps."

Each lamp illuminates an event in the history of the novel's circle staged through its other technical innovation, the dialogue method. James's emphasis on dialogue is inspired by the French writer Gyp, by opportunistic editors whose cries of "Dialogue, always dialogue!" sound "from far back," and by his persisting attachment to the dramatic mode. Dialogue in *The Awkward Age* is both form and content, with talk seen as a means of education and social mediation, as well as contamination, and the women who preside at conversation parlors as powerful arbiters, within limits.

In "The Method of Henry James," Virginia Woolf cited James's lamps metaphor, commenting, "One had almost rather read what he meant to do than read what he actually did," but if we "want to be rid of realism," this theory from the *Awkward Age* preface offers a way to go about it. As Woolf's comment indicates, James is as often classified among moderns like Joyce and Proust as he is among nineteenth-century realists like Eliot and Hardy. Inevitably, all of these writers themselves straddled such classifications. And some critics even view James as closer to late twentieth-century writers than to any from his own time. While the slipperiness of these categories tells us more about the need for them than about the writers they label, they help to explain James's longevity.

6. Like many intellectuals of his time, Henry James countered his sedentary writing and reading habits by taking exercise on his bicycle.

What makes James "modern" in an enduring sense is the originality that motivated his narrative style and development of genres like the novella. Then there is his abundant curiosity. Despite his reputation for insularity and traditionalism, James was attracted to novelty and to a range of creative technologies. He was an early user of the telephone and the typewriter (dictating his narratives after the rheumatism in his right hand worsened in 1897), was attending movies by the late 1890s, and enthusiastically procured the professional photographs of Alvin Coburn as frontispieces for his New York Edition.

While still in his twenties, Coburn was already well known for his expertise in the new art of the camera. Coburn and James met in the United States in 1905 when Coburn photographed the author for a magazine piece. James decided that the talented photographer might produce an image for each of his New York

Edition works, capturing a scene or an object associated with the location of the novel. Thus, for *The Ambassadors*, set in Paris, James suggested a picture of the Theatre Francais or the Luxembourg Gardens. For *The Princess Cassamassima* he wanted the dome of St. Paul's Cathedral in London, and for *The Portrait of a Lady*, an English country house and a Roman bridge.

In the 1898 novella *In the Cage*, James fictionalized the experiences of a young woman who operates a telegraph—a technology that might be viewed as the Internet of the nineteenth century. James's story is esteemed by leading analysts of media studies, who see it as anticipating the information network that has become predominant in our own era. The story's understanding of communication as always circuitous and heavily mediated, and its account of the telegraph operator's anonymous and unacknowledged passion for the gentleman she assists, seems especially prophetic. James's prescience about emerging technologies helps explain why his work has spoken to twenty-first-century theorists. Consider the following observation of his: "So much of the ingenuity of the world goes to multiplying contact and communication, to reducing separation and distance, to promoting, in short, an inter-penetration that would have been the wonder of our fathers."

The telegraph business was efficient and profitable for those who benefitted from it, because of the labor it enlisted, that of young women, who joined an army of female information workers—particularly typists, stenographers, and telephone switchboard operators. With Anthony Trollope, who wrote his own story about a "Telegraph Girl" (1877), James wonders about these independent young women equipped with specialized skills working in urban areas outside the domestic sphere: How do they maintain respectability? Whom do they marry? What makes *In the Cage* unique is that it invests an ordinary worker in the turn-of-the-century information economy with a classical Jamesian sensibility.

The novella's unnamed telegraphist is typical of James's heroines. She shares Isabel Archer's penchant for introspection and self-criticalness, tending similarly toward flights of fantasy that end in regret. She is full of insight into her surrounding world, and acutely sensitive about the discrepancies between elite and working-class life chances:

> She had early learnt that if you became a telegraphist you soon ceased to be astonished. Her eye for types amounted nevertheless to genius and there were those she liked and those she hated.... She was rigid in general on the article of making the public itself affix its stamps, and found a special employment in dealing to that end with some of the ladies who were too grand to touch them. She had thus a play of refinement and subtlety... and though most people were too stupid to be conscious of this it brought her endless small consolations and revenges.

The daughter of an alcoholic, the telegraphist is familiar with poverty and hunger, and appreciates the security afforded by a job and suitor, though Mr. Mudge, a grocery clerk, fails to stir her imagination. She is enough of a pragmatist and survivor, however, to accept that Mr. Mudge's limitations pale beside "the early times of their great misery, her own, her mother's and her elder sister's... they had slipped faster and faster down the steep slope at the bottom of which she alone had rebounded." Her closest friend is a widow "who had invented a new career for women— that of being in and out of people's houses to look after the flowers." Mrs. Jordan's plan to seize the opportunity afforded by her flower tending, her fond belief "that a single step more would transform her whole social position," sets the more guarded ambitions of the telegraphist in relief.

The telegraphist has her own dreams of social mobility, but in contrast to those of the voluble widow, hers are private. "Her imaginative life was the life in which she spent most of her time," and "one of her most cherished complaints" was "that people didn't understand her." It was "a matter of indifference to her that Mrs. Jordan shouldn't," though the latter was "the only member of her circle in whom she recognized an equal."

The great drama of the telegraphist's life comes when two aristocrats, Lady Bradeen and Captain Everhard, start frequenting her shop to send telegrams. Her absorption in their comings and goings leads her to imagine they are endangered, and also that they envision a role for her in the stratagems their telegrams support. "Her folly had gone to the point of her half-believing that the other party to the affair must sometimes mention in Eaton Square the extraordinary little person at the place from which he so often wired."

The telegraphist becomes involved with the pair, to the extent a clerk in such a position might. They grow accustomed to her adeptness, which is enhanced by her obsession with them. Eventually the telegraphist even takes a walk in the park with the exalted Everhard, which she regards as a momentous romantic event. The end result can only be disappointment, even tragedy, and the dashed expectations of the novella's protagonist approximate notably Émile Durkheim's theory of anomie, conceptualized in the 1890s.

Durkheim's theory proposes the danger of ambitions that exceed one's class position and capacity to realize them. Anomie is an expression of individual and social pathology that can lead to high rates of suicide. From the perspective of anomie, it is fitting that the narrative concludes with the telegraphist strolling ominously on a foggy bridge at night under the suspicious gaze of a policeman. Whether she is inclined to leap into the river below, or simply struggling to accept the terms of her constricted life, the ending is bleak.

To say that happy endings are a rarity for James is putting it mildly. The majority of his novels and novellas end in loss sweetened by the assurance of enlightenment. *The Altar of the Dead* and *The Beast in the Jungle* resemble *In the Cage* by depicting characters whose grim fate is to mistake the life of the mind for life itself.

But the more eventful *Aspern Papers* is no less devastating in the concluding blow it delivers its "publishing scoundrel" protagonist. Presumably based on an anecdote James heard about the Romantic poet-politician Lord Byron, the novella pits a biographer seeking the papers of a deceased writer against the writer's lover, who is impelled personally and through her role as executor to forbid access. The intervention of a niece, who becomes the biographer's manipulative ally, promising her uncle's private letters in exchange for the biographer's vow of marriage, comes to naught when the niece impulsively burns them all.

For James, what distinguished the novella was "the effort to do the complicated thing with a strong brevity and lucidity—to arrive, on behalf of multiplicity, at a certain science of control." The challenge was how to achieve such control without sacrificing his high aesthetic standards. *The Altar of the Dead*, for instance, had struck him at first as a perfect idea for a relatively concise treatment, but the more he worked on it the more it grew, finally topping eighteen thousand words.

The Beast in the Jungle is the most admired, and frequently anthologized, of his novellas, and it treats the quintessential Jamesian subject: anxiety and regret over a wasted life. In James, the biggest loss is neither unhappiness nor failure, but rather the avoidance of experience and connection with other human beings. Isabel Archer's unfortunate choice of husband; Olive Chancellor's predations; Kate Croy's foiled scheme to secure a fortune for herself and her lover—all of these acts, however productive of suffering, are preferable to the vacuum that is John Marcher's existence.

James seems to have taken the novella's nugget from Constance Fenimore Woolson. Woolson's outline reads: "To imagine a man spending his life looking for and waiting for his 'splendid moment.'...But the moment never comes." James complicates the situation with May Bartram's vicarious embrace of Marcher's watch. She bolsters his pride by substantiating the worth of his vigil, while providing companionship and love. This story of a man who devoutly withholds himself from ordinary experience as he awaits the distinguished fate he believes is his due has captured the imaginations of varieties of James critics. For some of his biographers, Marcher replicates his creator's own penchant for exploiting and then withdrawing from women friends.

The literary theorist Eve Sedgwick's "The Beast in the Closet" (1986) revolutionized James criticism by identifying Marcher's looming discovery as his lack of heterosexual, and terror of homosexual, desire. According to Sedgwick, May Bartram sees accurately that Marcher will never be able to live, let alone love, until he can abandon the closet and assume an appropriate identity, whether as a full-fledged homosexual man, or as someone with a more provisional sexuality.

Like any groundbreaking analysis, Sedgwick's gave rise to decades of revisionary James criticism, but it has also been resisted by critics persuaded that James's sexual proclivities escape definitive labeling. Whether James was the active homosexual fictionalized by Colm Tóibín in *The Master* (2004), or the celibate ascetic married to his art, as David Lodge conceived him in *Author, Author* (2004), remains irresolvable. And the author of *The Aspern Papers* undoubtedly intended that it would be.

The primary theme of *The Beast in the Jungle* is the hunger for individuality as a basic feature of the modern personality. Ambition, grandiosity, the conviction that he is special, different from the multitudes, is Marcher's chief, indeed only, characteristic. Otherwise he is a blank. May Bartram catches his attention

7. Henry James with his beloved dog, a purebred dachshund named Max, in the garden at Lamb House. James had pet dogs for most of his adult life.

because she remembers him, singles him out from "the crowd," though "he *really* didn't remember the least thing about her." What she has harbored for years is his secret "sense of being kept for something rare and strange, possibly prodigious and terrible."

Her gift to him is recognition of his unique destiny, something he expects no one else could understand:

> He wore a mask painted with the social simper out of the eyeholes of which there looked eyes of an expression not in the least matching the other features. This the stupid world, even after years, had never more than half discovered. It was only May Bartram who had…meeting the eyes from in front and mingling her own vision, as from over his shoulder, with their peep through the apertures…she did watch with him, and so she let this association give shape and color to her own existence.

As is often the case in James, echoes of Hawthorne prove telling. *The Scarlet Letter* haunts the novella, particularly at the end, with the image of "the garden of death" that "gave [Marcher] the few square feet of earth on which he could still most live." Hawthorne writes of Hester and Dimmesdale that "one tombstone served for both," while Marcher, in the final line of *The Beast in the Jungle*, standing before May Bartram's grave, "flung himself, on his face, on the tomb."

But the most pronounced echo is May's last declaration to Marcher that his sense of destiny had "done its office. It has made you all its own." The statement recalls Hawthorne's stern one-line paragraph: "The scarlet letter had not done its office," which proclaims that Hester has managed to subvert her punishment. James, as usual, strives to outdo Hawthorne with an even more extravagant fictional scheme. Where *The Scarlet Letter*, as James interpreted it, is the story of a transgression that has already occurred, and therefore "plotless," with the narrative beginning after the adultery has been committed, *The Beast in the Jungle* is a story propelled by the expectation of an event that never happens.

Marcher's final view of himself as "the man of his time, *the* man, to whom nothing on earth was to have happened," his recognition that the only escape from this fate would have been to love May

Bartram, who herself *has* lived by loving *him* for himself, suggests the persistence of his cleaving for distinction. Though he admits guiltily that "he had never thought of her...but in the chill of his egotism and the light of her use," such concessions do not indicate that he has grown in any way. For Marcher misunderstands that the cultivation of individuality can never be an end in itself, but is always a means: the more evolved the self, the greater its capacity for sociability. What's bestial in the story is not Marcher's craving for individuality per se, but his inability to recognize its relational purpose.

And this is where James the author parts ways with his tragically flawed character. James thought deeply about the ways in which avoiding human connection impoverished experience, and much of that thinking bears fruit in this magnificent story. The chasm between James and the elaborately represented consciousness of his protagonist is confirmed as well by the way the description of the mask Marcher wears in public foreshadows James's description of "The House of Fiction" in the preface to *The Portrait of a Lady*. Marcher overlooks how much he needs May Bartram "mingling her own vision," to "peep through the apertures" with him.

But James never forgot that "The House of Fiction" was an expression of human heterogeneity that could only be captured by the relational artist, forever striving to connect to others through empathic imagining of their experience. James, in contrast to his character John Marcher, did take risks, embrace compromise, make choices, and suffer on behalf of his art. And he never lost sight of the author's dependence on readers, a reliance that kept his enterprise humane. *The Beast in the Jungle* is James's allegory about the sociability of the authorial enterprise.

Chapter 5
Masterpieces

Among the achievements of James's professional career is the remarkable brevity of the time span—1902 to 1904—during which he wrote the three novels generally considered his greatest: *The Wings of the Dove* (1902), *The Ambassadors* (1903), and *The Golden Bowl* (1904). These fictions were followed by a major travel narrative, *The American Scene* (1907), which was based on a tour he took throughout the United States in 1904–5, where he gave lectures and interviews expounding on topics of contemporary interest.

The travel narrative and the opinions that it staged prove James to be a man of his time, betraying prejudice and discontent befitting an expatriate of his class and age. The masterpieces, in contrast, reveal a universal artist, a novelist with insights into the deepest human dilemmas. *The Ambassadors* is a meditation on the nature of ambition, destiny, and what makes a life meaningful. The subject of *The Wings of the Dove* is illness and suffering, and the moral conundrum presented by a dying girl possessed of great wealth she cannot enjoy and her needy friends who seek to inherit it. *The Golden Bowl* is about the institutions of marriage and family, and the way they are disrupted by passion: the passion of fathers and daughters, husbands and wives, and lovers. Each of these works builds on a typical Jamesian concern: the international plot of *The Ambassadors*, the themes of manipulation and deceit in *The Wings of the Dove*, the examination of social norms and their violation in *The Golden Bowl*.

Of his many fictions, *The Ambassadors* was James's favorite. "The book is intrinsically, I dare say, the best I have written," he divulged to a regular correspondent, the novelist Mrs. Humphry Ward, in 1903. Critics have concurred, with F. O. Matthiessen venturing it "the most skillfully planned novel ever," and Philip Fisher writing, "perhaps from an academic point of view the most perfect book ever written by an American." Based on emotional advice delivered by William Dean Howells—"*live*. Live all you can: it's a mistake not to"—presumably overheard by another friend, the anecdote stayed with James for years before he was able to make something of it.

James commented in a Notebook entry on October 31, 1895, "It touches me...it suggests a little situation...the figure of an elderly man who hasn't 'lived,' hasn't at all, in the sense of sensations, passions, impulses, pleasures.... He has never really enjoyed—he has lived only for Duty and conscience." As with the actor Marlon Brando's famous lament from *On The Waterfront* ("I coulda been a contender, I coulda been *some*body"), anyone can identify with Strether's sense of lost possibility; this is why the novel has so many admirers.

Once James got to work he was relentless, producing for prospective magazine editors in October 1900 a 20,000-word "Project of Novel by Henry James," which was so detailed it threatened to overwhelm the subsequent writing process. As he noted at the end of this document, "The difficulty with one's having made so very full a Statement as the present is that one seems to have gone far toward saying *all*: which I needn't add that I haven't in the least pretended to do." The novel was written in a white heat; by August 10, 1901, James was reporting to William Dean Howells that *The Ambassadors* was finished and that Howells was himself "responsible for the whole business." The difficulty James's agent, James Pinker, had in placing *The Ambassadors* as a serial resulted in the earlier publication of *The Wings of the Dove*, written just as rapidly (once James began work in earnest) on the heels of *The Ambassadors*. *Wings* was published as a book in August 1902, and serialization of *The Ambassadors* in the *North American Review* began in January 1903.

The plot of *The Ambassadors* is relatively simple. A reflective middle-aged American is commissioned by a close friend, Mrs. Newsome (whom he hopes to marry) to go to Paris and rescue her son, Chad, who seems to have lost his way among the dazzling attractions of the French capitol. The Newsomes are upstanding citizens who have made a fortune through manufacturing a small domestic object. James tactfully refrains from naming the object, out of ostensible respect for the pride of his leading family. The suggestion is that the product is possibly coarse or distasteful, or perhaps that its triviality undermines the dignity of the Newsome's commercial dynasty.

What happens to James's "ambassador" is the novel's chief dramatic action. Arriving in Paris, he finds that, far from corrupted, the twenty-eight-year-old Chad is notably improved by his Parisian sojourn. After meeting the thirty-eight-year-old French lady responsible for Chad's refinement—whether through lovemaking or grooming as a prospective son-in-law, or both— Strether concludes that Madame de Vionnet is "the person of most personal charm, indisputably, that" he "has ever met." She seems to represent "most of the things that make the *charm* of civilization…civilization." His enchantment allows him to overlook the fact that she is the estranged wife of a count and that any dalliances she might pursue are by definition extramarital.

The bare bones of plot, however, convey little, for as James forewarns in his "Project," the telling is all. One of the novel's first critics, Percy Lubbock, observed, "Strether's real situation, in fact, is not his open and visible situation, between the lady in New

England and the young man in Paris; his grand adventure is not expressed in its incidents. These, as they are devised by the author, are secondary, they are the extension of the moral event that takes place in the breast of the ambassador, his change of mind." Moreover, the reader "is placed in a better position for understanding…Strether's history" than "Strether himself."

The "change of mind" to which Lubbock refers is Strether's attitude toward his delegated task and the commercial and provincial values underpinning it. Success would entail Chad's return to command both the family business and "a large share of its profits," and to marry a suitable young New England bride. It is Strether's desire to embrace life in all of its complexity that proves far stronger than the ultimately quite conventional impulses of Chad Newsome.

Indeed, Strether's almost constitutional wistfulness compromises his errand from the start. It takes less than two days—"under forty-eight hours"—in Paris for him to begin "feeling the general stirred life of connexions long since individually dropped…the vast bright Babylon like some huge iridescent object, a jewel brilliant and hard, in which parts were not to be discriminated nor differences comfortably marked.…It was a place of which, unmistakably Chad was fond; wherefore if he, Strether, would like too much, what on earth…would become of either of them?"

Strether is the classic James protagonist, reluctant to surrender his innocence as he plunges into a world utterly at odds with it. Despite his mature conviction of lost time and opportunity, the glacial pace of his grasp of the novel's moral quagmire (which partly explains the singularly protracted narrative) is naïve and signals how sheltered his life has been. Still, Strether's growth, however slow, offers a pronounced contrast to the absence of any such transformation in the young man he is sent to rescue. The only way Chad has changed, *could* change, is physically.

Upon meeting him, Strether is struck by the fact that "Chad had been made over," had "been put into a firm mould and turned successfully out.... He saw him in a flash as the young man marked out by women." But Chad turns out to be a philistine whose sojourn in Paris is only that. When Strether tells him near the novel's end that the Pococks, the second set of ambassadors enlisted by Mrs. Newsome, were sent not "to see for themselves what you're doing, but what I'm doing...it was me, in other words, they were after," he is pinpointing the reversal that has occurred.

Chad's rescuer is the one who needs rescuing, in the novel's deepest lights from his narrow Woollett existence. The tragedy of the novel is not that Chad returns, but that Strether does. The novel's titular metaphor is plural, because emissaries so often go astray—missions get foiled, upended, and inverted, and delegates lose their will or sense of purpose. What happens to Strether is that he is seduced by Paris and by Chad's adulterous partner Madame de Vionnet, in that order, and also by the image of their love. And through this he is given a view of how rich and intricate life can be.

The scene where he "discovers" them on a visit to the country, drifting together on a boat, their amorous bond unmistakable as air, is the novel's most famous. Before recognizing the man and woman as Chad and Madame de Vionnet, Strether recognizes their profound familiarity, "that they were expert...that this wouldn't at all events be the first time." Their guilt is confirmed by their dissembling; Strether sees that "they would show nothing if they could feel sure he hadn't made them out.... It was a sharp fantastic crisis that had popped up as if in a dream."

After sharing the remainder of the day with the exposed lovers, Strether is left alone to contemplate the magnitude of their deception. His first response is moral indignation: it was "the quantity of make-believe involved...that most disagreed with his spiritual stomach." But indignation soon turns to envy and Strether's default setting—his sense of deprivation. "The deep, deep truth of the intimacy revealed. That was what, in his vain vigil, he oftenest reverted to: intimacy, at such a point was *like* that." It "made him feel lonely and cold."

His desolation is not the only tragic dimension of the novel's ending. Madame de Vionnet's anguish opposes Strether's condition like a distorted mirror. Unlike Strether, she *has* risked passion; loving Chad as she does makes the imminent loss of him earth-shattering. "Embroider as she might and disclaim as she might—what was at bottom the matter with her was simply Chad himself. It was of Chad she was after all renewedly afraid; the strange strength of her passion was the very strength of her fear; she clung to *him*." Strether is almost in awe of "the passion, mature, abysmal, pitiful, she represented."

In this Strether recalls John Marcher in the graveyard in *The Beast in the Jungle* confronting a man in the stranglehold of grief, knowing that his own sorry fate is never to have felt such emotion. *The Ambassadors* also recalls *The American*, avenging the story of Christopher Newman—the entrepreneurial young American in Paris armed with his ethic of commerce and profit while dabbling in something more—by granting Chad Newsome the French woman of his dreams and allowing him to reject her in one swift undramatized departure.

Yet the novel belongs to Strether, and it is his consciousness, his insight that matters most. Where Marcher has sacrificed his life for a myth, Strether, as a superior Jamesian protagonist, a ruminator, a thinker, can be expected to sup heartily ever after upon what he has witnessed in Paris.

In his preface to *The Wings of the Dove*, James points to the "memory...very old" and "motive," "very young" that seems always to have been "vividly present to me." The story "of a young person conscious of a great capacity for life, but early stricken and doomed, condemned to die under short respite...long had I turned it over, standing off from it, yet coming back to it; convinced of what might be done with it, yet seeing the theme as formidable." James's provocation is both personal and professional. The death of a young woman with everything to live for recalls the fate of James's beloved cousin from his youth, Mary "Minny" Temple, who died of tuberculosis at the age of twenty-four. It also satisfied the writer Edgar Allan Poe's notorious claim from "The Philosophy of Composition," that the death of a beautiful woman was "the most poetical topic in the world."

As with all of his works, it is the characters and plot that James devises for his original inspiration that makes all the difference. The narrative centers upon an ambitious and appealing young Englishwoman, Kate Croy, who is determined to overcome the disadvantages of a shabby upbringing consisting of a defeated mother and wastrel father. But Kate is in love with a journalist, Merton Densher, who is without means, and *Wings* hinges on the London arrival of Milly Theale, a wealthy American heiress with a deadly illness who has fallen in love with Densher during a trip he takes to New York. Ethical considerations aside, the solution from Kate's perspective is obvious: Densher should conceal his devotion to Kate and court Milly, thus ensuring the ailing girl a few happy last months and a return to Kate with the capital to marry her properly. From this marvelously succinct scheme is woven a narrative of incomparable complexity.

The novel's guiding concern is illness and death, and the peculiar power accorded those who suffer its debilitating effects. Confronting death, James understood, aroused elemental fears on the part of individuals and communities. He was familiar with studies of ancient civilizations that perceived any death as a threat to the larger collective survival. Because it was so imperiling, so awesome, death, among these ancients, required an explanation, the identification of a cause or a culprit. James builds on these kinds of associations in *Wings* by making the tragic death of Milly Theale a story about the relationship between innocents and plotters, which are linked implicitly, by the novel's title, to the crucifixion of Christ. For the title comes from Psalm 55: "O that I had wings like a dove / Then I would fly away and be at rest / For it was not an enemy that reproached me / But it was thou / My companion and familiar friend."

The idea of Milly Theale as a Christ betrayed was the main focus of early criticism on *The Wings of the Dove*. Related to this standard Christian reading is the novel's melodramatic donnée— an 1894 notebook entry sketch for the stage. In this early variation on the novel's themes, Milly was a pathetic doomed innocent, Kate was a greedy villain, and the plot was catalyzed by the simple formula of deceit, betrayal, and death. The formula was a mainstay of James's "melodramatic imagination," which is exemplified by an 1896 letter to A. C. Benson, provost of Magdalene College, Cambridge, where James confesses, "I have the imagination of disaster and see life as ferocious and sinister."

In the words of his secretary, Theodora Bosanquet, when James "walked out of the refuge of his study into the world and looked about him, he saw a place of torment, where creatures of prey perpetually thrust their claws into the doomed, defenseless children of light." Throughout his career, James created fictions representing powerful characters who make "conveniences" of others—Madame Merle, Kate Croy—and the more ostensibly passive characters who allow them to—Isabel Archer, Milly Theale.

The exploitative nature of human interaction is explored in *The Wings of the Dove* more fully than in any of James's fiction and informs how language is deployed. When Milly Theale announces early in the narrative, "I want abysses," she affirms her bona fides as a James character, and also that she is in the right novel. For *Wings* has gained over the years a notoriety for what it *fails* to represent: the devastating encounter between Milly and Lord Mark (where he divulges the long-standing intimacy of Kate and Densher) whose result is Milly's "turn[ing] her face to the wall," making his divulgence a literal death sentence; Kate and Densher's sexual tryst; the final meeting of Milly and Densher; Milly's letter containing her bequest to Densher and Kate, which amounts to "the turn she" gives "her act." As these many examples suggest, all the novel's protagonists wield narrative and linguistic control; no one character monopolizes the construction or labeling of events and people.

Though Milly is often read by critics as a victim of Kate and Densher's stratagems, she proves equally adept at manipulating them. The scene where Kate pronounces Milly "a dove," for instance, shows how Milly manages—despite her gracious acceptance of it—to reconfigure the appellation. Milly "felt herself ever so delicately, so considerately embraced; not with familiarity or as a liberty taken, but almost ceremonially and in the manner of an accolade, partly as if, though a dove who could perch on a finger, one were also a princess with whom forms were to be observed." In light of Milly's recasting of Kate's inspiration, it is critical that it is preceded by Milly's private designation of Kate as "a panther." Because it is secret, Milly's naming of Kate goes unchallenged. Throughout the novel James insists on a mutuality of exchange among his characters, that any assertion or coercion is partial and liable to qualification. To inhabit his worlds is to know how to navigate intrigue. Indeed, because they are underestimated, apparent innocents often end up most in control.

The Wings of the Dove is renowned for its difficulty as a reading experience, but it also acquired quite a following among a range of literary lights. In a free-wheeling reminiscence about James's career, the American cartoonist James Thurber recalled an evening during the 1930s in a Manhattan bar when the mystery writer Dashiell Hammett "suddenly startled us all by announcing that his writing had been influenced by Henry James's novel, 'The

Wings of the Dove.'" The work also made a strong impression on the author Owen Wister, who considered it exemplary of James's unique storytelling method. "One grows used to it by persisting," he advised, for James "does not undertake to tell a story but to deal with a situation, a single situation. Beginning at the center of this situation, he works outward, intricately and exhaustively, spinning his web around every part of the situation, every little necessary part no matter how slight, until he gradually presents to you the organic whole, worked out...he never lets the situation go, never digresses for a single instant; and no matter how slow or long his pages may seem as you first read them, when you have at the end grasped the total thing, if you then look back you find that the voluminous texture is woven closely and that every touch bears upon the main issue."

James's exquisite design is centered on the heroine, Kate Croy, whose experience frames the action. Beginning and ending with Kate, the narrative emphasizes her embattled obligations to demanding, dysfunctional kin:

> She waited, Kate Croy, for her father to come in, but he kept her unconscionably, and there were moments at which she showed herself, in the glass over the mantel, a face positively pale with the irritation that had brought her to the point of going away without sight of him. It was at this point, however, that she remained.... Each time she turned in again, each time, in her impatience, she gave him up, it was to sound to a deeper depth...the failure of fortune and of honour.

Kate wisely recognizes that familial freight must be dealt with if she has any hope of moving on. Repeatedly she affirms her father's impossibility and repeatedly she affirms the necessity of confronting him. Similarly, Kate learns from the straitened circumstances of her sister—"if that was what marriage necessarily did to you"—that economic security is the basis of the good life.

Kate's commitment to dealing directly with contingencies, her refusal to see herself as immune to the misfortunes of others, provides her route to freedom. But this courage would be fruitless without the gift for overcoming limitations that she quite literally embodies, possessing, "stature without height, grace without motion, presence without mass." It is this amplitude and self-assurance that makes her appealing to Densher, who is the opposite: "Young for the House of Commons, he was loose for the Army. He was refined, as might have been said, for the City, and quite apart from the cut of his cloth, skeptical, it might have been felt, for the Church. On the other hand he was credulous for diplomacy, or perhaps even for science, while he was perhaps too much in his mere senses for poetry and too little in them for art." Constitutionally ambivalent, Densher resists any real prospect of a vocation. The enticements of a decisive lover are obvious, but even more essential is a wealthy spouse.

Enter Milly with her sadness, oddity, and millions, the ideal supplement to Kate and Densher. Milly is introduced poised before a precipice, "the dizzy edge of it . . . a slab of rock at the end of a short promontory or excrescence that merely pointed off to the right at gulfs of air." From here, "in a state of uplifted and unlimited possession," she contemplates "the kingdoms of the earth. . . . Was she choosing among them or did she want them all?" Despite the hint of avidity, suicide seems the stronger urge, planting the idea that Milly's appetite for life is weaker than those of the other protagonists. Standing before the sixteenth-century painting by the Italian Bronzino, which James describes in the novel, Milly acknowledges what everyone has already noticed, her unmistakable resemblance to Lucrezia Panciatichi, the portrait's subject. The fact that this "very great personage," as Milly phrases it, is "dead, dead, dead," enhances the inevitability of her own looming fate. Yet Milly also confirms at this moment the power of art to preserve the dead.

8. This photograph by Alice Boughton, who developed a reputation for photographing major literary and theatrical figures, was taken in 1906. James had a keen appreciation for the visual arts, as evidenced by his friendships with artists and attention to visual detail in his novels.

Her conviction is rewarded by the novel's ending, which pictures James's ultimate fantasy of immortality in the form of Milly's triumphant afterlife. As in *The Turn of the Screw*, the dead exert control over the living through their preservation in the memories of those who loved them. Now fully the Dove, Milly offers her gift to Kate and Densher on Christmas Eve, enfolding them in a mantle that aggressively divides as much as it protects or conjoins. For Densher is unable to accept Kate with Milly's money, while Kate is unable to marry Densher without it. The ever practical Kate will move on with the wealth, the ever-temporizing Densher will maintain a shrine, paying worshipful homage to the dead Milly while compulsively recalling his sexual tryst with Kate.

The Wings of the Dove is a major novel in part because of the subjects it manages to fictionalize so memorably: illness, death, and the ethics of inherited wealth. *The Golden Bowl* is even more ambitious, with its exploration of marriage in the context of economy and nationality: the exchange of men and women, and of commodities like the Golden Bowl, and the relationship of gift-giving and capitalist enterprise to the state of the declining British and rising American empires. The novel is set primarily in London and features a handsome Italian prince, Amerigo, from a family of celebrated ancestry without wealth; an American man of business, Adam Verver, wealthy beyond compare but kinless except for his daughter, Maggie, who has all that money can buy; and Charlotte Stant, an admired American older friend of Maggie's from boarding school, extraordinary in every way but financially insecure.

The novel begins with preparations for the marriage of Amerigo and Maggie. Maggie's mother is long dead, and Maggie worries about leaving Verver. Though her marriage barely alters their life together, it enhances Verver's eligibility from the perspective of eager single women, which leads Maggie to resolve that he should marry Charlotte. Maggie and Verver are unaware of the previous love affair between Charlotte and Amerigo, abandoned on the recognition that their mutual poverty precludes marriage.

The Ververs's obsession with each other—the novel's "open secret"—prevents their noticing the lingering attraction between Charlotte and Amerigo, known only to the Assinghams, who have helped to arrange Maggie's marriage. Marriage, as figured in the eponymous bowl itself, is slightly damaged, cracked. Vended by a mildly sinister Jew, who keeps it ceremonially apart from the other bric-a-brac in his shop, the bowl binds the novel's social and racial plot—centered on the state of the empire and the aliens who threaten it—with the novel's familial plot—centered on the curious pairings, incestuous and adulterous, among the protagonists.

Everything in *The Golden Bowl*—from princes, friends, husbands, fathers, and daughters to tiles, precious art, and dinner invitations—is marketable. The novel is preoccupied with the condition of the Anglo-American empire and the social and sexual form considered crucial to its preservation—heterosexual marriage. James's favorite topic—wealth versus poverty; rich people buying poor people—becomes part of a comprehensive study of marriage, and with it the exploration of male versus female natures and the different ways in which the passions and appetites of men and women support and threaten the social order. As with all of James's great works, what makes the novel compelling is the characters, each of them invested with the author's empathetic insight.

Charlotte Stant is a representative Jamesian consciousness. Among the qualities that make her attractive to the prince is her capacity for appreciating human particularity in everyone, high or low: "Her own vision acted for every relation—this he had seen for himself; she remarked beggars, she remembered servants, she recognized cabmen; she had often distinguished beauty, when out with him, in dirty children; she had admired 'type' in faces at hucksters' stalls. Therefore, on this occasion, she had found their 'antiquario' interesting; partly because he cared so for his things, and partly because he cared—well, so for 'them.'"

The other female lead, Maggie Verver, is aligned with James in her awe and fear of power. Toward the novel's end she contemplates the four lives she could destroy (hers included) through public exposure of the prince and Charlotte's revived affair. "She found herself for five minutes, thrilling with the idea of the prodigious effect that, just as she sat there near them, she had at her command.... There reigned for her, absolutely, during those vertiginous moments, that fascination of the monstrous, that temptation of the horribly possible." Her companions "might have been figures rehearsing some play of which she herself was the author.... They might in short have represented any mystery they would; the point being predominantly that the key to the mystery...was there in her pocket."

Amerigo is a ladykiller, who liked "to mark them off, the women to whom he hadn't made love: it represented—and that was what pleased him in it—a different stage of existence from the time at which he liked to mark off the women to whom he had." Maggie's craving for her husband is the novel's driving force. "She never admired him so much, or so found him heart-breakingly handsome, clever, irresistible, in the very degree in which he had originally and fatally dawned upon her, as when she saw other women reduced to the same passive pulp that had then begun, once for all, to constitute *her* substance." Her cruelty is aroused by protecting what she believes to be hers. Thus, Maggie orchestrates Charlotte's exile to the American wilderness the latter detests, "a long silken halter looped round her beautiful neck," its end held "in one of [Verver's] pocketed hands." Maggie's declaration to her husband, "It's...*always* terrible for women," rings false in applying only to women who can't afford their passion.

Then there is the haunting, bilingual Jew, who eavesdrops on the Italian conversation of Charlotte and Amerigo, discovering their intimacy before the Ververs themselves. He subsequently sells the Golden Bowl, passed over by the lovers, to Maggie for her father's birthday present. The dealer is aligned with the prince as an Italian speaker and also through their respective conversions in Book Two. While the prince rededicates himself to marriage, the dealer reveals the crack in the bowl to Maggie, acting "on a scruple rare enough in vendors of any class, and almost unprecedented in the thrifty children of Israel."

This slur on the bowl dealer is consistent with the depiction of the Jewish tile merchant, a Mr. Gutermann-Seuss, whose progeny, "eleven little brown clear faces, yet with such impersonal old eyes astride of such impersonal old noses," contrast menacingly with the one-child family of Maggie and Amerigo. The stereotypes of *The Golden Bowl* align with the contradictory aspersions on Jewish identity in James's time: the idea of Jews in Anglo-America as archaic but highly adaptable to a modern system of exchange.

There is nothing necessarily Jewish, however, about the continuity of ancient ritual with modern times. Adam Verver, for instance, stages the ties between capitalist profiteering and primitive reciprocity. Giving is for him a way of keeping. A gift that is not matched by a counter-gift creates a permanent asymmetry, restricting the debtor's freedom. Verver plans to build a museum in American City with "all the sanctions of civilization . . . a house from whose open doors and windows, open to grateful, to thirsty millions, the higher, the highest knowledge would shine out to bless the land. In this house, designed as a gift, primarily, to the people of his adoptive city and native State, the urgency of whose release from the bondage of ugliness he was in a position to measure—in this museum of museums, a palace of art . . . a receptacle of treasures sifted to positive sanctity."

Verver's power is reinforced by his giving, which enables further acquisition. Everything, to him, is subject to appropriation, even loved ones. His daughter recalls a "slim draped 'antique' of Vatican or Capitoline halls, late and refined, rare as a note." His new grandson is like "precious small pieces he had handled." Maggie is a chip off the old block, as confirmed by her final view of Amerigo and Charlotte: "high expressions of the kind of human furniture required, aesthetically, by such a scene...concrete attestations of a rare power of purchase." The novel's attention to ancient exchange rituals (the prince's early ruminations about marriage, the image of the bowl vendor displaying "the touch of some mystic rite of old Jewry") serves to bring out its most prominent theme: the "basic imperialism" of human relations.

By marrying Maggie Verver to Prince Amerigo and Adam Verver to Charlotte Stant, James marks gift-giving—the sharing of one's fortune with "the poor" as the basis of marriage—while also identifying marriage as the typical transactional form. And with not one but two Jewish merchants presiding over transactions preceding each marriage, James asserts the interdependence of social aliens and marriage.

In *The Golden Bowl*, Jews symbolize survival and adaptation, a culture which has endured since ancient times that is equally associated with capitalist economics. Aligned with primitive rites as well as a threatening modernity, Jews are a social element analogous to adultery in marriage. As adultery is to marriage, Jews are to society—transgressive and distasteful, but necessary. Amerigo's infidelity fortifies his marriage to Maggie, while Jewish aliens play leading roles in exchange rites essential to marriage.

James's portrait of Jews in *The Golden Bowl* is relatively subtle and complex, but there is little subtlety in the ethnic stereotypes that fill *The American Scene* (1907). James's famous travelogue on his native land can be a challenge for literary analysts who prefer authors they admire to share their enlightened opinions. James's critics have responded variously to what seems unabashed elitism and prejudice.

Such elements are unmistakable. James's return to the United States following a twenty-year absence intensified anxieties about his native land that had motivated his self-exile. Between his arrival in Hoboken, New Jersey, in August 1904 through the early summer of 1905, when he sailed back to England, James visited old stomping grounds (Manhattan, Boston, Concord, Newport) and places he had never been (the "Confederate" South) testing his memories and theories against the profoundly transformed actuality he encountered.

James's title for *The American Scene* might well have been "The Return of the Native," except that Thomas Hardy had used it years earlier. James had been away so long that he almost felt like a Rip Van Winkle, if not a foreigner himself. Some of his travels involved catching up with old friends and family. The night of his arrival he was the guest of his publisher George Harvey, along with fellow author Mark Twain, and he spent a long visit with his brother William in Chocorua, William's summer home in New Hampshire. He caught up with the writer Henry Adams in Washington, the art collector Elizabeth Stuart Gardner in Brookline near Boston, and the novelist Edith Wharton in Lenox, Massachusetts.

James managed to make the tour profitable by giving public lectures, including the controversial "The Question of Our Speech," at the Bryn Mawr commencement in June 1905. While the address has been remembered as an indictment of American speech, it is as much a call to arms that privileges *how* things are said over content, and encouraged the female student audience to become "models and missionaries" of clarity and eloquence. James also funded his journey by publishing most of the manuscript in magazines ahead of its 1907 publication as a book. Ten of *The American Scene*'s fourteen chapters were published from 1905 to

1906 in the *North American Review*, *Harper's Monthly*, and the *Fortnightly Review*.

Much of what James discerns of his rediscovered country is acute. He finds the impact of "creative destruction" everywhere: a "perpetual repudiation of the past, so far as there had been a past to repudiate." But he finds little in the way of compensations for this rejection of tradition. He has "seen many persons," but he has encountered "no personages." He has "heard much talk—but no conversation." Worst of all, his compatriots have no idea of what they are missing. The art of living is nowhere to be found.

This is the consequence, James observes, of the prevailing American maxim: "To make so much money that you won't, that you don't 'mind,' don't mind anything—that is absolutely, I think, the main American formula.... This basis is that of active pecuniary gain and of active pecuniary gain only." The paradox is how useful this maxim turns out to be for the incorporation of others, making the country an unusually elastic organism for assimilating refugees from foreign lands.

But even more important is James's insistence that most "strangers" are hardly strange at all, at least not in America, where being from elsewhere is a fundamental national characteristic. He appreciates that all Americans are different in a country composed like no other of waves upon waves of immigrants, where being different from others is the norm. "Who and what is an alien, when it comes to that, in a country peopled from the first under the jealous eye of history?—peopled, that is, by migrations at once extremely recent, perfectly traceable, and urgently required.... Which is the American by these scant measures?—which is *not* the alien, over a large part of the country at least, and where does one put a finger on the dividing line?"

Yet this very openness is both cause and result of what James misses most. Just as he laments the passion for novelty that makes everything susceptible to demolition, he mourns the distinctive attributes and manners that require centuries of history to produce. Only two representative groups prove resistant to absorption: Jews, the most prominent aliens in the book, and Blacks.

"The individual Jew," James writes, is "more of a concentrated person, savingly possessed of everything that is in him, than any other human," while the collectivity, "the whole hard glitter of Israel," testifies to "the extent of the Hebrew conquest of New York." Despite occasional qualification, James's rhetoric is punctuated with references to race, zoology, hygiene, and deceit, culminating with a question: "Who can ever tell, moreover...what the genius of Israel may, or may not, really be 'up to'?"

Blacks are subject to more extreme disparagement. James's honorable mention of the Black sociologist and public intellectual W. E. B. Du Bois's *The Souls of Black Folk*, "by that most accomplished member...of the negro race," does little to mitigate harsh references to the "deep-seated inaptitude of the negro race at large for any alertness of personal service," or statements like "the negro had always been, and could absolutely not fail to be, intensely 'on the nerves' of the South."

It is lamentable that James's vast understanding did not extend to empathy for two groups that have over the centuries been more unjustly subject than any others to stereotyping, discrimination, and violence. Such limitations are one with a certain narrowness in his work—the charges of elitism and snobbery, the contention that the stories and novels he produced are hardly "everyone's cup of tea." Yet there is no disputing that there was something powerfully humane in James, a spark that enabled his imagination of characters and plots with an incomparable originality. To note that his work sometimes registered a lack of enlightenment consistent with views shared by many writers and intellectuals of his time is to affirm that he was human.

Epilogue

In the first decade of his career, James declared, "Nothing is my *last* word about anything—I am interminably super subtle and analytic—and with the blessing of heaven, I shall live to make all sorts of representations of all sorts of things." The remarks anticipate James's penchant for revision, the habit of perfecting his works tirelessly, never quite willing to let go. They also reflect the ambition that his literary contributions will be able to exploit the range of possibilities afforded by his cultural moment. And they confirm a dogged secularism—God was never a point of reference for him. Perhaps most intriguingly, they prophesy his posthumous fame, the fact that his opus has felt malleable to subsequent readers and artists, susceptible to appropriation and reconceptualization.

James endures in the twentieth and twenty-first centuries as a phenomenon as much as any writer of his time, with his life and personality, and his writings, consistently subject to creative reimagining. Hence the trend whereby James becomes the main character of fictions loosely based on his biography, as well as the extensive adaptation of his work for film and TV. While the popularity James craved mostly eluded him, he would have appreciated the irony of a rich afterlife.

9. This 1913 portrait of Henry James by John Singer Sargent was commissioned by a group of James's friends for his seventieth birthday. Sargent and James were great admirers of each other's work, and Sargent was an obvious choice despite having largely given up portraiture by that time.

The persisting attractions of James's life and works undoubtedly has something to do with their rarity and difficulty. To identify with James, to profess partiality for his singular fiction, has been a means of establishing cultural literacy. For many writers and intellectuals, James represents high culture, and affirming one's loyalty to and affinity for the Master and his writings is to establish a certain aesthetic worthiness. Yet the frequent film and TV adaptations of James's writings suggest that his appeal is prompted by more than elitism. An exhaustive bibliography estimates there to be 125 screen works of 46 James fictions. Though the practice of adapting novels by classic authors for cinematic treatment is routine (consider the Jane Austen film industry) and suggests a high demand for compelling plots and characters, there is no question that filmmakers have been especially drawn to James.

One explanation is how the intimacy of the screen suits James's focus on inward drama. An obliqueness that was not congenial to theater has proven readily amenable to film. The habit of making points through long looks and uninterrupted meditative sessions in front of fireplaces works very well cinematically, often better than speech or dialogue, though James's work provides plenty of fine samples of the latter as well.

There is also the durability of his themes: the position of women, the multifariousness of human sexuality, and the problem of knowledge. James's keen awareness of class and money and his understanding of how wealth confers power through social connections and networks have become ever more relevant in our era of super capitalism, when the divide between rich and poor is more extreme, and the existence of vast fortunes amassed on a global stage have made the Gilded Age tycoons of his time seem modest by comparison.

Yet another source of James's contemporaneity is his commitment to literary innovation, to theory and method. His choice to use Alvin Coburn photographs as frontispieces for the New York Edition of his collected works was an expression of his openness to new visual forms. His broad aesthetic interests, including his lifelong immersion in painting and the other arts, extended to fascination with the potential of modern types of visuality, including film. At the time when James was preparing the New York Edition, mainstream cinema was refining many of its standard production and narrative conventions.

Of the nineteen most renowned English-language films based on James stories and novels, *The Turn of the Screw* tops the list with six adaptations. The producer-director team Merchant-Ivory made five James novels into films, and leading directors who have worked on adaptations include Peter Bogdanovich, Jane Campion, Agnieszka Holland, François Truffaut, Michael Winner, and William Wyler. Anglo-American stars have performed in the films: Montgomery Clift as Morris Townsend and Olivia de Havilland as Catherine, with Ralph Richardson playing Dr. Sloper, in the 1949 William Wyler version of *Washington Square*; Deborah Kerr portrayed the governess in the 1961 version of *The Turn of the Screw*, directed and produced by Jack Clayton; and Marlon Brando was Peter Quint in Michael Winner's 1971 *Turn of the Screw*. In Jane Campion's 1996 *The Portrait of a Lady*, Nicole Kidman was Isabel Archer; Barbara Hershey, Madame Merle; Viggo Mortensen, Caspar Goodwood; and John Malkovich, Gilbert Osmond; and in 1997's *The Wings of the Dove*, Helen Bonham Carter played Kate Croy and Charlotte Rampling portrayed Aunt Maude.

One of the challenges of adapting James is the difficulty of capturing his irony on film. For James loyalists, schooled in his senses of irony and ambiguity, the pleasure of watching film versions of his work is assessing the gap between the novels and their visual adaptations. Earnestness and excessive adherence to the James original are probably the least useful impulses for an adaptor; filmmakers redoing great novels do best when they are equipped with strong sensibilities and a measure of irreverence. Such inclinations most closely approximate James's own leanings, given his alertness to cultural change and fascination with the cutting edge. This is why Jane Campion's *The Portrait of a Lady* might, in its own distinctive way, be the most faithful of recent approaches.

A strong artist in her own right, Campion's feminism helps to pinpoint James's own. Both the novelist and the director recognize the role played by young women as spectacles, and how their respective genres—novel and film—exploit that cultural objectification. Drawing on Ralph Touchett's conviction that his cousin Isabel represented "entertainment of a high order...finer than the finest work of art—than a Greek bas-relief, than a great Titian, than a Gothic cathedral," Campion's *Portrait* presents the aesthetic scrutiny and appropriation of women as both fundamentally cinematic and fundamentally Jamesian.

What makes Campion's film successful is the grasp of the contrasts between novelistic and film methodologies she builds into her *Portrait*. That bodies rather than words are the medium of film is emphasized by the introductory image where the film's title is literally inscribed on the flesh—the finger—of a young woman. Next Campion challenges the classic subjection of women to the film gaze with a series of girls staring directly back at the camera, thus defusing their objectification.

The film proceeds in this way, reminding us that while Isabel Archer's sexuality and ultimate fate are products of character and culture, they are also determined by the many who take an interest in her, from male figures such as Daniel and Ralph Touchett, Lord Warburton, Caspar Goodwood, and Gilbert Osmond, to a varied cast of women, including Mrs. Touchett, Madame Merle, Henrietta Stackpole, and Pansy Osmond. In the end, the film pleased neither James aficionados nor theatergoers. And here the significance of Jamesian ambiguity is paramount. For James is able, through narrative technique and interior monologues—and even through irony at Isabel's expense—to establish the complexities of her fate, revealing her as simultaneously a victim of the culture and of her own independence. Lacking these nuances of language and tone, Campion's film, in contrast, leaves viewers mystified about what motivates Isabel and brings about her ultimate unhappiness.

The attempt to translate James into film is at least in part about filling in spaces left to the imagination in the works themselves. Films set characters in stone, whether the actors are famous or obscure; they pinpoint scenes and setting; and they dramatize incidents and encounters left deliberately opaque (sex especially). Recent biographical fiction shares the tactic of spelling out experiences James kept private. As Lyndall Gordon has asserted, "Everything in James—fictions, reviews, and memoirs—suggests that documentary truth is limited and needs the complement of imaginative truth." Instead of letting readers pursue this "imaginative truth" themselves, the James fictions, as if presuming the disappearance of his readership or seeking to hurry it along, provide their own versions of it for the masses.

To be sure, some of these accounts seem designed to expand James's reputation, while those by Joyce Carol Oates, Colm Tóibín, and Cynthia Ozick, in particular, invest the past of an esteemed forebear with each writer's memorable stamp. It's worth emphasizing that author fictions are not all that new. Consider Homer's portrayal of the poet Democdocus in *The Odyssey* or Dante's of Virgil in his *Divine Comedy*. Writers have long paid homage to predecessors in this fashion. Nor is James the only "modern" author to figure in fiction. Poe, Flaubert, Dickinson, Wilde, Woolf, and Plath, to mention a few, have all appeared as protagonists in novels, some of them more than once. James himself was fascinated by the appetite for authors' lives, which he explored notably in *The Aspern Papers*.

At the start of the third decade of the twenty-first century, there were about two dozen novels featuring James as a character. The year 2004 could be viewed as a banner year, because multiple examples of these fictions were published. David Lodge has suggested that the genre is either "a sign of decadence and exhaustion in contemporary writing," or "a positive and ingenious way of coping with the 'anxiety of influence.'" For Lodge, recounting his surprise when three James novels (by Tóibín, Alan Hollinghurst, and Emma Tennant) came out in 2004, along with his own *Author, Author*, the anxiety extended to the crowded field of biographical fiction.

The dominant conceit differs for each. In Alan Hollinghurst's *The Line of Beauty*, for example, the protagonist is a James disciple rather than James himself, and the setting is London in the 1980s. Nick Guest, the protagonist-narrator, is a young gay man writing a dissertation on James and a screenplay of *The Spoils of Poynton*. Emma Tennant's James is a patriarchal snob, dismissive of his close companion Constance Fenimore Woolson while incapable of realizing his homoerotic leanings. Tennant's book, titled *Felony*, depends, like others of the genre, on Lyndall Gordon's *A Private Life of Henry James*, and is concerned with the writing of *The Aspern Papers* and the Florentine woman, Claire Clairmont, who presumably provided the story's donnée.

Tóibín's *The Master* is regarded as the best novelization of James, largely because it recreates James's world with fidelity and tact. In contrast to some of these works, Tóibín avoids imposing anachronistic behaviors and leaves much of what goes on in the mind of his subject to the imagination. Hewing closely to Gordon's *A Private Life*, Tóibín invests a biographical portrait he admired but found overly critical with greater empathy. Where Gordon's James erects a strict divide between himself and intimates to defend his art and professional obligations, Tóibín's is less deliberate and more vulnerable in his withdrawals.

As John Updike noted, *The Master*'s "extensive, misty, and intricate work of reconstruction" is "a marvel of lightly worn research and modulated tone." It succeeds by channeling James, indeed so expertly that the book reads like the biographical fiction

James might have written had he produced one of his own. Whether or not real intimacy was a problem for James, Tóibín manages to engage intimately with the author, which makes his choices appear uniquely appropriate.

Thus, *The Master*'s starting point, a crisis—the failure of *Guy Domville*—seems inevitable, as does the concentration on signature moments between 1895 and 1900. Leon Edel labeled these "The Treacherous Years" in his five-volume biography, and it is a sign of the resilience Tóibín finds in James that the time span ends with him ensconced at Lamb House alone, plying his craft. The writer in Tóibín appreciates James's rededication to what he did best, following the failure of the playwriting career he so desired.

Above all, Tóibín knows what peace and quiet can mean to a writer:

> He loved the glorious silence a morning brought, knowing that he had no appointments that afternoon and no engagements that evening. He had grown fat on solitude, he thought, and he had learned to expect nothing from the day but at best a dull contentment. Sometimes the fullness came to the fore with a strange and insistent ache, which he would entertain briefly, but learn to keep at bay. Mostly, however, it was the contentment he entertained; the slow ease and the silence could, once night had fallen, fill him with a happiness that nothing, no society nor the company of any individual, no glamour or glitter, could equal.

Tóibín understands the requirements of the writing life, the curious pleasures provided by isolation and loss. While James had many disappointments, and the poor sales of the collected New York Edition of his works was the next major professional blow, the solace he could take in his own company and in the life of the mind was a continual salvation. It is also in *The Master* a sign of courage. What Tóibín sees in James above all is the same "bravery"

Tóibín's James attributes to Isabel Archer's return to Rome at the end of *Portrait of a Lady* in conversation with his adolescent niece Peggy, who laments the decision. Being obligated to an ideal, a goal, even one that is trying, is for James as important as being obligated to others. Isabel Archer returns for the benefit of Pansy, but she also returns for herself, convinced that what she is doing is right. James recognized his good fortune in having a vocation that could confer that sense of rightness. All that was needed was an ability to savor isolation instead of fearing it.

In an essay on Walter Benjamin, Peter Brooks offers insights into the power of novelistic art. Novels are struggles against time whose meanings derive from duration: characters age, choose wisely and unwisely, and learn. "What readers look for in the novel is that which is inaccessible to them in their own lives: the knowledge of death. It is with the end of life that its meaning becomes apparent. And that is what we seek in the death (which may be figurative but is preferably literal) of the fictional character."

James's own death was a dramatic one, replete with Napoleonic overtones suitable to a creator who guided many from life to death. Alice James, William's widow (he had died of a heart condition on August 26, 1910), presided over Henry's final months. Between December 2, 1915, and February 16, 1916, James had multiple strokes and drifted in and out of consciousness. He had been reading Napoleon's memoirs in 1915 and had even met some Bonaparte descendants. James's affinities—of physiognomy and character—with this symbol of military authority is a recurrent motif in Edel's biography, whose climax is James's remarkable ventriloquism of the French general on his deathbed. Arriving on March 1, 1916, with the Master already in his coffin, Theodora Bosanquet said, "Several people who have seen the dead face are struck with the likeness to Napoleon which is certainly great."

While he was often incoherent, there were instances of clarity when he dictated complete letters from Napoleon to his two

10. Henry James (far right) toured the United States in 1904–5 to write *The American Scene*. This photograph is from a visit to his brother William, William's wife, Alice, and their daughter, Peggy, at the James family house on Irving Street in Cambridge, Massachusetts.

sisters, down to the detail of the correct Corsican spelling— "Napoleone"—of the name. The letters had instructions on decorations for palaces as well as the Louvre and the Tuileries, expressing hopes for the future of "our young but so highly considered Republic." At times, the Napoleon persona gave way to James himself, and then the recollections featured automobile tours with Edith Wharton, and friends such as Fanny Kemble, Robert Louis Stevenson, and Henry Adams.

Of these last words, none was more moving than the charge to nephew Billy and his whole generation of young men: "Tell them *to follow, to be faithful, to take me seriously.*" On the last point,

James needn't have worried. On January 1, 1916, fifty-nine days before his death, James's admission to the Order of Merit was announced, an honor bestowed previously upon only two other writers, Thomas Hardy and George Meredith.

The memorandum to the prime minister recommending James conceded that he "is sometimes blamed for dealing only with characters drawn from the hothouse life of the leisured classes, hypertrophied in intellect and emotion," but notes that his "infinitely expressive" style "is one of the most individual that has ever been evolved," and that "no writer of his time gives the same impression of knowledge and mastery in the architectural structure of his works."

The memorial service in Chelsea Old Church, a site favored by literary figures, was described by the English author Sir Edmund Gosse in a letter to the *Times*: "We stood around the shell of that incomparable brain, of that noble and tender heart, it flashed across me that…He was a supreme artist; but what we must remember and repeat is that he was a hero…an English hero of whom England shall be proud." The memorial plaque to James placed in the Old Chelsea Church reinforced this national claim. But he was not yet home.

Per James's request, the body was cremated at the new London crematorium, Golders Green, and the ashes were transported back to Cambridge, Massachusetts, by his sister-in-law, Alice. Because it was wartime, Alice smuggled the remains past Customs. The urn filled with the ashes of Henry James reached its final resting place in the James family plot in Cambridge Cemetery. A single red-brick wall, with the James surname inscribed at the apex, encompasses six headstones. That of Henry James Jr. stands between those of his mother, Mary, and sister, Alice. It reads: "Henry James, OM, Novelist, Citizen of Two Countries, Interpreter of His Generation on Both Sides of the Sea."

References

Prologue

Henry James, *The Portrait of a Lady* (New York: Penguin, 1979), 5, x–xi.

William Dean Howells, "Henry James Jr." *The Century* 25 (November 1882), 28.

William James quoted in F. O. Matthiessen, *The James Family* (New York: Knopf, 1947), 338.

Carolyn Porter, "Gender and Value in *The American*" (anonymous quote within), in *New Essays on "The American,"* ed. Martha Banta (New York: Cambridge University Press, 1987), 99.

Donald Barthelme, *Snow White*, quoted in John Carlos Rowe, *The Theoretical Dimensions of Henry James* (Madison: University of Wisconsin Press, 2009), 8.

Ruth Yeazell quoted in *Henry James: A Collection of Critical Essays*, ed. Leon Edel (New York: Prentice Hall, 1994), 13.

Seymour Chatman, *The Later Style of Henry James* (Oxford: Basil Blackwell, 1972), 30, 109.

Henry James, "Preface," in *The Wings of the Dove* (Oxford: Oxford University Press, 1984), xlvi.

Henry James to James Pinker, ed. Philip Horne, *Henry James: A Life in Letters* (New York: Penguin, 2001), 543.

Henry James, *Hawthorne* (New York: Collier, 1966), 139, 125.

William James quoted in F. O. Matthiessen, *The James Family* (New York: Knopf, 1947), 69.

Henry James, "Standard Biography," in *The Portrait of a Lady* (New York: Penguin, 1979).

Lyndall Gordon, *A Private Life of Henry James* (New York: Norton, 1998), 134.

Henry James, *A Small Boy and Others* (New York: Macmillan, 1913), 315, 316.

William James quoted in F. O. Matthiessen, *The James Family* (New York: Knopf, 1947), 303.

Chapter 1

William James, *The Letters of William James* (New York: Atlantic Monthly Press, 1920), 2.

Henry James, *A Small Boy and Others* (New York: Macmillan, 1913), 200.

Lyndall Gordon, *A Private Life of Henry James* (New York: Norton, 1998), 10–11.

William Dean Howells and Ralph Waldo Emerson quoted in Leon Edel, *Henry James: The Untried Years* (New York: Avon, 1978), 36, 40, 59, 63.

Henry James quoted in Leon Edel, *The Untried Years* (New York: Avon, 1978) 59, 63.

E. L. Godkin quoted in F. O. Matthiessen, *The James Family* (New York: Knopf, 1947) 74, 75–76, 71.

Ralph Waldo Emerson quoted in Leon Edel, *The Untried Years* (New York: Avon, 1978), 34.

F. O. Matthiessen, *The James Family* (New York: Knopf, 1947), 101, 14, 70.

Henry James, *A Small Boy and Others* (New York: Macmillan, 1913), 232, 227, 246.

Henry James, *Notes of a Son and Brother* (New York: Macmillan, 1914), 180, 120, 344.

Lyndall Gordon, *A Private Life of Henry James* (New York: Norton, 1998), 41.

Jean Strouse, *Alice James: A Biography* (New York: NYRB Classics, 2011), 52–53.

Henry James and Edith Wharton quoted in F. O. Matthiessen, *The James Family* (New York: Knopf, 1947), 490–92, 489.

Mary James to Henry James, July 26, 1872, James Papers, Harvard University.

William James and William Dean Howells quoted in Michael Anesko, *Friction with the Market: Henry James and the*

Profession of Authorship (New York: Oxford University Press, 1986), 38, 37, 44.

Henry James to William James, *Henry James Letters,* Vol. II (Cambridge, MA: Harvard University Press, 1975), 179.

Michael Anesko, *Friction with the Market: Henry James and the Profession of Authorship* (New York: Oxford University Press, 1986), 168.

Susan L. Mizruchi, *The Rise of Multicultural America* (Chapel Hill: University of North Carolina Press, 2008).

William James quoted in F. O. Matthiessen, *The James Family* (New York: Knopf, 1947), 323, 319.

Henry James, *Hawthorne* (New York: Collier, 1966), 18.

Henry James to Grace Norton, quoted in Fred Kaplan, *Henry James: The Imagination of Genius* (Baltimore: Johns Hopkins University Press, 1992), 187.

E. L. Godkin and Henry James quoted in Fred Kaplan, *Henry James: The Imagination of Genius* (Baltimore: Johns Hopkins University Press, 1992) 187, 220.

Henry James, *Hawthorne* (New York: Collier, 1966), 47–48, 53, 25.

T. S. Eliot, "In Memory," "The Hawthorne Aspect," "Henry James Number," *The Little Review,* August 1918, 46, 52.

Henry James, *Hawthorne* (New York: Collier, 1966), 100, 99, 91, 89, 151.

Nathaniel Hawthorne, *The Scarlet Letter* (New York: Penguin, 1983), 61–62.

Henry James, *The Portrait of a Lady* (New York: Penguin, 1979), 25.

D. H. Lawrence, *Studies in Classic American Literature* (New York: Thomas Seltzer, 1923), 3.

Henry James, *Henry James: Literary Criticism: French Writers, Other European Writers, the Prefaces to the New York Edition* (New York: Library of America, 1984) 11, 41.

Henry James, *Henry James: Literary Criticism: Essays on Literature, American Writers, English Writers* (New York: Library of America, 1984), 1141, 1143, 1145.

Henry James, *Henry James: Literary Criticism: French Writers, Other European Writers, the Prefaces to the New York Edition* (New York: Library of America, 1984), 1011, 48, 972, 973, 974, 975, 996, 998.

Henry James, *Henry James: Literary Criticism: Essays on Literature, American Writers, English Writers* (New York: Library of America, 1984), 6, 7, 8–9, 639–40.

Lyndall Gordon, *A Private Life of Henry James* (New York: Norton, 1998), 213.

Henry James, *Henry James: Literary Criticism: French Writers, Other European Writers, the Prefaces to the New York Edition* (New York: Library of America, 1984), 866.

Henry James, *Henry James: Literary Criticism: Essays on Literature, American Writers, English Writers* (New York: Library of America, 1984) 856–57, 1048, 958, 959, 960, 965, 966.

Henry James, *The Europeans* (New York: Penguin, 1979), 5, 7.

Henry James, "Daisy Miller," in *"The Turn of the Screw" and Other Short Novels* (New York: Signet, 1962), 129,164, 144, 110–111, 129.

William T. Stafford, *James's Daisy Miller: The Story, the Play, the Critics* (New York: Scribners, 1963), 164.

Henry James, *Washington Square* (New York: Library of America, 1990), 3, 5, 8, 9, 38, 79–80, 81.

Henry James, *The Portrait of a Lady* (New York: Penguin, 1979), 432.

Henry James, *Washington Square* (New York: Library of America, 1990) 94–95, 173.

Chapter 3

Henry James, *Hawthorne* (New York: Collier, 1966), 139, 125.

Henry James to Thomas Perry, September 20, 1867, ed. Philip Horne, *Henry James: A Life in Letters* (New York: Penguin, 2001), 17.

Roy Harvey Pearce, Introduction to *The American* (New York: Riverside, 1962), vi, vii.

Henry James to William James, October 29, 1888, *The Letters of Henry James* (New York: Scribners, 1920), 141.

Henry James, "The Art of Fiction," in *Henry James: Literary Criticism: Essays on Literature, American Writers, English Writers* (New York: Library of America, 1984), 45.

Henry James to William Dean Howells, quoted in *New Essays on "The American,"* ed. Martha Banta (New York: Cambridge University Press, 1987), 6.

Henry James to Henry James Sr., December 20, 1875, *Henry James Letters*, Volume II (Cambridge, MA: Harvard University Press, 1975), 15.

Henry James, *The American* (New York: Riverside, 1962), 20, 326–27.

Henry James, "Preface to *The American*," in *Henry James: Literary Criticism: French Writers, Other European Writers, the Prefaces to the New York Edition* (New York: Library of America, 1984), 1054, 1060–61.

Michiko Kakutani, "Henry James's Criticism," *New York Times*, January 26, 1985, Section 1, Page 13.

Henry James, "The Art of Fiction," in *Henry James: Literary Criticism: Essays on Literature, American Writers, English Writers* (New York: Library of America, 1984), 46, 50, 51, 52, 53, 56, 57, 58, 64.

Henry James, *The Portrait of a Lady* (New York: Penguin, 1979), 46.

R. P. Blackmur, *Studies in Henry James* (New York: New Directions, 1983), 193.

Henry James, *The Portrait of a Lady* (New York: Penguin, 1979), 405, 35, 50, 51, 25, 164, 48, 578–79, 561, 577.

Henry James, "Preface to *The Portrait of a Lady*," in *Henry James: Literary Criticism: French Writers, Other European Writers, The Prefaces to the New York Edition* (New York: Library of America, 1984), 1080, 1081, 1075.

Henry James, "Preface to *The Golden Bowl*," in *Henry James: Literary Criticism: French Writers, Other European Writers, The Prefaces to the New York Edition* (New York: Library of America, 1984), 1332.

Colm Tóibín, "Introduction," in *The Art of the Novel* (Chicago: University of Chicago Press, 2011), xi–xii.

Henry James, "The Question of the Opportunities," in *Henry James: Literary Criticism: Essays on Literature, American Writers, English Writers* (New York: Library of America, 1984), 653.

Chapter 4

Leon Edel, *Henry James: The Master* (Philadelphia: Lippincott, 1972), 301–2.

John Dewey quoted in F. O. Matthiessen, *The James Family* (New York: Knopf, 1947), 587.

Willard Thorp, "Foreword," in *"The Turn of the Screw" and Other Short Novels: Henry James* (New York: Signet, 1962), vi.

Horace Elisha Scudder, "Review of *The Bostonians*," *Atlantic Monthly* 57 (June 1886), 852.

Henry James, *The Bostonians* (New York: Penguin, 1978), 216.

Henry James, *The Notebooks of Henry James* (Chicago: University of Chicago Press, 1981), 47.

Henry James, *The Bostonians* (New York: Penguin, 1978), 56, 108, 163, 371, 388, 389.

Henry James to Robert Louis Stevenson, January 12, 1891, *The Letters of Henry James* (New York: Scribners, 1920), 176.

Henry James to William James, December 29, 1893, *The Letters of Henry James* (New York: Scribners, 1920), 211.

Henry James, *The Notebooks of Henry James* (Chicago: University of Chicago Press, 1981), 178.

William James quoted in F. O. Matthiessen, *The James Family* (New York: Knopf, 1947), 590.

Henry James, *The Turn of the Screw*, ed. Peter G. Beidler (New York: Bedford/St. Martins, 1995), 11–12, 25, 27.

Henry James, *The Awkward Age* (New York: Penguin, 1981), 9, 10, 89, 111, 118, 204, 195, 205, 260, Preface, 17, Preface, 14.

Virginia Woolf, "The Method of Henry James," *Times Literary Supplement*, December 26, 1918.

Henry James, *Henry James: Literary Criticism: Essays on Literature, American Writers, English Writers* (New York: Library of America, 1984), 664.

Henry James, *Eight Tales from the Major Phase: "In the Cage" and Others* (New York: Norton, 1969), 188, 176, 177, 211.

Henry James, "Aspern Papers," in *"The Turn of the Screw" and Other Short Novels: Henry James* (New York: Signet, 1962), 233.

Henry James quoted in Introduction to *"The Turn of the Screw" and Other Short Novels: Henry James* (New York: Signet, 1962), xi, ix.

Lyndall Gordon, *A Private Life of Henry James* (New York: Norton, 1998), 286, 364.

Henry James, "The Beast in the Jungle," in *"The Turn of the Screw" and Other Short Novels: Henry James* (New York: Signet, 1962), 404, 407, 411, 419.

Nathaniel Hawthorne, *The Scarlet Letter* (New York: Penguin, 1983), 275.

Henry James, "The Beast in the Jungle," in *"The Turn of the Screw" and Other Short Novels: Henry James* (New York: Signet, 1962), 451.

Nathaniel Hawthorne, *The Scarlet Letter* (New York: Penguin, 1983), 184.

Henry James, "The Beast in the Jungle," in *"The Turn of the Screw" and Other Short Novels: Henry James* (New York: Signet, 1962), 450, 419.

Chapter 5

Henry James to Mrs. Humphrey Ward, December 16, 1903, *Henry James: A Life in Letters* (New York: Penguin, 2001), 391.

F. O. Matthiessen and Phillip Fisher quoted in *The Ambassadors*, Norton Critical Edition (New York: Norton, 1994), 429, 536.

Henry James quoted in *The Ambassadors*, Norton Critical Edition (New York: Norton, 1994), 429, 408, 374–75.

Henry James, "Project of Novel," in *The Ambassadors*, Norton Critical Edition (New York: Norton, 1994), 404.

Henry James to William Dean Howells, quoted in *The Ambassadors*, Norton Critical Edition (New York: Norton, 1994), 406.

Henry James, "Project of Novel," in *The Ambassadors*, Norton Critical Edition (New York: Norton, 1994), 388–389.

Percy Lubbock, "Point of View in *The Ambassadors*," in *The Ambassadors*, Norton Critical Edition (New York: Norton, 1994), 417, 418.

Henry James, *The Ambassadors*, Norton Critical Edition (New York: Norton, 1994), 62, 64, 95–96, 97, 98, 286–87, 309, 310, 315, 324, 325.

Henry James, *The Wings of the Dove*, Norton Critical Edition (New York: Norton, 1978), 3.

Edgar Allan Poe, "The Philosophy of Composition," in *Essays and Reviews* (New York: Library of America, 1984), 19.

Henry James to A.C. Benson, June 29, 1896, *Henry James: Letters to A.C. Benson and Auguste Monod* (London: E. Mathews & Marrot, 1930), 35.

Theodora Bosanquet quoted in Peter Brooks, *The Melodramatic Imagination: Balzac, Henry James, Melodrama, and the Mode of Excess* (New Haven, CT: Yale University Press, 1995), 5.

Henry James, *The Wings of the Dove* (New York: Norton, 1978), 120, 333, 359, 398, 171.

Dashiell Hammett quoted in James Thurber, "The Wings of Henry James," *New Yorker*, October 30, 1959.

Owen Wister quoted in James Thurber, "The Wings of Henry James," *New Yorker*, October 30, 1959.

Henry James, *The Wings of the Dove* (New York: Norton, 1978), 21, 41, 22, 45–46, 87, 137.

Henry James, *The Golden Bowl* (New York: Penguin, 1973) 99, 456–57, 458, 42, 138, 493, 534, 449, 124–25, 153, 126, 541.

Marcel Mauss, *The Gift* (New York: Norton, 1990), 65.

Henry James, "The Question of Our Speech," in *"The Question of Our Speech" and "The Lesson of Balzac"* (New York: Houghton Mifflin, 1905), 52.

Henry James, *The American Scene* (London: Chapman and Hall, 1907), 53–54.

Henry James to Grace Norton, December 13, 1881, *Henry James Letters*, Volume II (Cambridge: Harvard University Press, 1975), 365.

Henry James, *The American Scene* (London: Chapman and Hall, 1907), 236, 124, 132, 135, 418, 423, 376.

Epilogue

Henry James to Jane D. F. Hill, June 15, 1879, ed. Philip Horne, *Henry James: A Life in Letters* (New York: Penguin, 2001), 104.

J. Sarah Koch, "A Henry James Filmography," in *Henry James Goes to the Movies*, ed. Susan Griffin (Lexington: University Press of Kentucky), 337.

Henry James, *The Portrait of a Lady* (New York: Penguin, 1979), 63.

Lyndall Gordon, *A Private Life of Henry James* (New York: Norton, 1998), 370.

David Lodge quoted in J. Russell Perkin, "Imagining Henry: Henry James as a Fictional Character," *Journal of Modern Literature* 33 (Winter 2010), 118.

John Updike, "Silent Master," *New Yorker*, June 20, 2004.

Colm Tóibín, *The Master* (New York: Scribners, 2004), 45.

Peter Brooks, "The Story of the Story of the Story," *New York Review of Books*, January 16, 2020.

Theodora Bosanquet quoted in Leon Edel, *Henry James: The Master* (Philadelphia: Lippincott, 1972), 561.

Leon Edel, *Henry James: The Master* (Philadelphia: Lippincott, 1972), 561, 549–54.

Henry James quoted in Leon Edel, *Henry James: The Master* (Philadelphia: Lippincott, 1972), 554.

Memorandum to Prime Minister, quoted in Leon Edel, *Henry James: The Master* (Philadelphia: Lippincott, 1972), 555–56.

Edmund Gosse, quoted in Leon Edel, *Henry James: The Master* (Philadelphia: Lippincott, 1972), 561–62.

Further reading

Works by Henry James

The Ambassadors. New York: Norton, 1994.

The American. New York: Riverside, 1962.

The American Scene. London: Chapman and Hall, 1907.

The Awkward Age. New York: Penguin, 1981.

The Bostonians. New York: Penguin, 1978.

Eight Tales from the Major Phase: "In the Cage" and Others. New York: Norton, 1969.

The Europeans. New York: Penguin, 1979.

The Golden Bowl. New York: Penguin, 1973.

Hawthorne. New York: Collier, 1966.

The Letters of Henry James, ed. Leon Edel, Volume I: *1843–1875*. Cambridge, MA: Harvard University Press, 1974.

The Letters of Henry James, ed. Leon Edel, Volume II, *1875–1883*. Cambridge, MA: Harvard University Press, 1975.

The Letters of Henry James, ed. Leon Edel, Volume III, *1883–1895*. Cambridge, MA: Harvard University Press, 1980.

The Letters of Henry James, ed. Leon Edel, Volume IV, *1895–1916*. Cambridge, MA: Harvard University Press, 1984.

Literary Criticism: Essays on Literature, American Writers, English Writers. New York: Library of America, 1984.

Literary Criticism: French Writers, Other European Writers, the Prefaces to the New York Edition. New York: Library of America, 1984.

The Notebooks of Henry James ed. Francis Otto Matthiessen and Kenneth Murdock. Chicago: University of Chicago Press, 1981.

Notes of a Son and Brother. New York: Macmillan, 1914.

The Portrait of a Lady. New York: Penguin, 1979.

The Princess Casamassima. New York: Penguin, 1987.

"The Question of Our Speech" and "The Lesson of Balzac." New York: Houghton Mifflin, 1905.

Selected Letters, ed. Leon Edel. Cambridge, MA: Harvard University Press, 1987.

A Small Boy and Others. New York: Macmillan, 1913.

"The Turn of the Screw" and Other Short Novels. New York: Signet, 1962.

Washington Square. New York: Library of America, 1990.

The Wings of the Dove. New York: Norton, 1978.

Secondary Works

Biography

Bosanquet, Theodora. *Henry James at Work*. London: Hogarth Press, 1924.

Edel, Leon. *Henry James: A Life*. 5 vols. New York: Avon, 1978.

Feinstein, Howard. *Becoming William James*. Ithaca, NY: Cornell University, 1984.

Gordon, Lyndall. *A Private Life of Henry James*. New York: Norton, 1998.

Habegger, Alfred. *The Father: A Life of Henry James, Sr*. New York: Farrar, Straus and Giroux, 1994.

Hollinghurst, Alan. *The Line of Beauty*. London: Picador, 2004.

Horne, Philip. *Henry James: A Life in Letters*. New York: Penguin, 2001.

Kaplan, Fred. *Henry James: The Imagination of Genius*. Baltimore: Johns Hopkins University Press, 1992.

Lodge, David. *Author, Author*. New York: Viking, 2004.

Matthiessen, Francis Otto. *The James Family: A Group Biography*. New York: Knopf, 1947.

Novick, Sheldon. *Henry James: The Mature Master*. New York: Random House, 2007.

Novick, Sheldon. *Henry James: The Young Master*. New York: Random House, 1996.

Ozick, Cynthia. *Dictation: A Quartet*. New York: Houghton Mifflin, 2008.

Strouse, Jean. *Alice James: A Biography*. New York: Bantam Books, 1982.

Tóibín, Colm. *The Master*. New York: Scribner, 2004.

Selected Criticism

Anesko, Michael, *Friction with the Market: Henry James and the Profession of Authorship*. New York: Oxford University Press, 1986.

Bentley, Nancy. *Frantic Panoramas: American Literature and Mass Culture, 1870–1920*. Philadelphia: University of Pennsylvania Press, 2009.

Blair, Sara. *Henry James and the Writing of Race and Nation*. Cambridge: Cambridge University Press, 1996.

Brodhead, Richard H. *The School of Hawthorne*. New York: Oxford University Press, 1986.

Brooks, Peter. *The Melodramatic Imagination: Balzac, Henry James, Melodrama, and the Mode of Excess*. New Haven, CT: Yale University Pres, 1995.

Cameron, Sharon. *Thinking in Henry James*. Chicago: University of Chicago Press, 1989.

Chatman, Seymour. *The Later Style of Henry James*. Oxford: Basil Blackwell, 1972.

Freedman, Jonathan. *Professions of Taste: Henry James, British Aestheticism, and Commodity Culture*. Stanford, CA: Stanford University Press, 1991.

Geismar, Maxwell. *Henry James and His Cult*. London: Chatto, 1964.

Griffin, Susan ed. *Henry James Goes to the Movies*. Lexington: University Press of Kentucky, 2002.

Habegger, Alfred. *Henry James and the "Woman Business."* Cambridge: Cambridge University Press, 1989.

Hale, Dorothy J. *Social Formalism: The Novel in Theory from James to the Present*. Stanford, CA: Stanford University Press, 1998.

Holland, Laurence B. *The Expense of Vision: Essays on the Craft of Henry James*. Baltimore: Johns Hopkins University Press, 1982.

Horne, Philip. *Henry James and Revision*. Oxford: Clarendon Press, 1990.

Johnson, Kendall. *Henry James and the Visual*. Cambridge: Cambridge University Press, 2007.

Krook, Dorothea. *The Ordeal of Consciousness in Henry James*. Cambridge: Cambridge University Press, 1962.

McWhirter, David. *Henry James New York Edition: The Construction of Authorship*. Stanford, CA: Stanford University Press, 1995.

Mizruchi, Susan L. *The Rise of Multicultural America: Economy and Print Culture, 1865–1915*. Chapel Hill: University of North Carolina Press, 2008.

Mizruchi, Susan L. *The Science of Sacrifice: Literature and Modern Social Theory*. Princeton, NJ: Princeton University Press, 1998.

Posnock, Ross. *The Trial of Curiosity: Henry James, William James, and the Challenge of Modernity*. Oxford: Oxford University Press, 1991.

Rivkin, Julie. *False Positions: The Representational Logics of Henry James's Fiction*. Stanford, CA: Stanford University Press, 1996.

Rowe, John Carlos. *The Theoretical Dimensions of Henry James*. Madison: University of Wisconsin Press, 2009.

Sedgwick, Eve Kosofsky. *The Epistemology of the Closet*. Berkeley: University of California Press, 1990.

Seltzer, Mark. *Henry James and the Art of Power*. Ithaca, NY: Cornell University Press, 1984.

Seymour, Miranda. *A Ring of Conspirators: Henry James and his Literary Circle, 1895–1915*. London: Hodder, 1988.

Yeazell, Ruth Bernard. *Language and Knowledge in the Late Novels of Henry James*. Chicago: University of Chicago Press, 1976.

Index

Note: Photographs are indicated by page numbers in *italics*.

Index

Index